Estes Park

PAST AND PRESENT

ESTES PARK

PAST

AND PRESENT

By JUNE E. CAROTHERS

THE UNIVERSITY OF DENVER PRESS

This Book Is Gratefully
Dedicated to

MY MOTHER AND FATHER

Welcome to Estes Park

One of the most charming resorts to be found in the Rocky Mountain West is Estes Park. Located in Colorado some sixty miles northwest of Denver, the Park was discovered in 1859 by Joel Estes. Since that day Estes Park has grown in popularity until today it has become a haven for pleasure seekers the world over. Although during the winter the population is numbered in the hundreds, during the summer it increases by the thousands. Fishing, horseback riding, mountain climbing, a marvelous climate, and beautiful scenery are the attractions which draw these visitors to the Park.

A place so well known to thousands of visitors could not fail to have a fascinating past as well as an interesting present. Such colorful characters as Isabella Bird, Rocky Mountain Jim, and the Earl of Dunraven have crossed the pages of Estes Park history. Their stories are also the stories of the settlers such as the Jameses, Spragues, MacGregors, Fergusons and later the Stanleys, Bonds, and the many others who have created the Estes Park of today. Now Estes Park is no longer a pioneer park but, rather, is a modern, thriving community.

To you who are interested in Estes Park and its people, I ask that you turn to the story of *Estes Park: Past and Present.*

June E. Carothers
Denver, Colorado
June, 1951

5

Acknowledgments

It is impossible for me to express adequately my sincere gratitude to the many people who have aided and encouraged me in writing this book. My heartfelt thanks go to Prof. H. G. Van Sickle, who guided the research for my Master of Arts thesis, "The Early History of Estes Park," and to Dr. Alan Swallow, who guided the transformation of that thesis into *Estes Park: Past and Present*.

Special thanks go to Miss Frances Shea, Miss Ina T. Aulls, Mrs. Alys Freeze, Mrs. Opal Harber, Dr. Le Roy R. Hafen, and Mrs. Dolores C. Renze who have been so helpful in locating materials for me. To David H. Canfield, Edwin C. Alberts, J. Barton Herschler, Ernest K. Field, Mrs. Ora Carr, Glenn Prosser, Carl B. Sanborn, and Mary Morris go my thanks for answering my many questions.

My special gratitude for the illustrations to the Matthews Studio and Clatworthy Studios of Estes Park, the Denver Public Library Western Collection, and the W. H. Jackson Collection of the State Historical Society of Colorado; to Craig Schafer for the map and to the Hancock Studio of Loveland for the cover picture.

Last but not least, my thanks go to my parents who have read and criticized my work and to the members of the University of Denver Press staff who have so painstakingly produced this book.

6

Contents

Illustrations

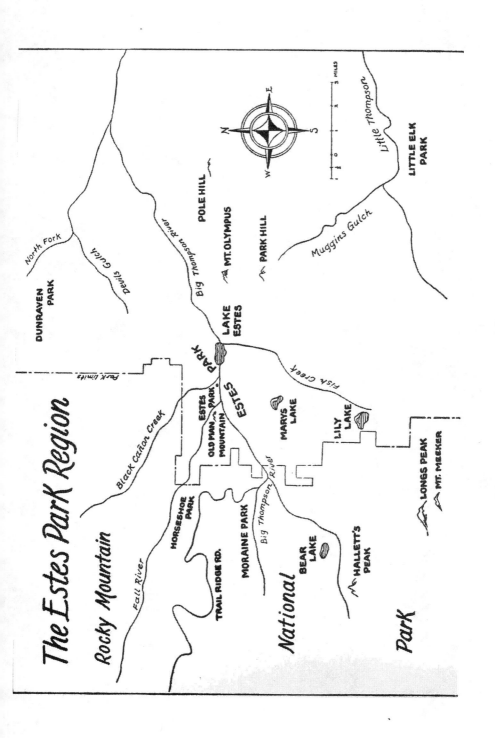

The Estes Park Region

Rocky Mountain

National

Park

DUNRAVEN PARK

North Fork

Devils Gulch

Fall River

Black Cañon Creek

Park limits

HORSESHOE PARK

TRAIL RIDGE RD.

MORAINE PARK

Big Thompson River

BEAR LAKE

HALLETT'S PEAK

LONGS PEAK

MT. MEEKER

ESTES

PARK

OLD MAN MOUNTAIN

ESTES PARK

MARYS LAKE

LILY LAKE

Big Thompson River

POLE HILL

MT. OLYMPUS

PARK HILL

LAKE ESTES

Fish Creek

Muggins Gulch

Little Thompson

LITTLE ELK PARK

N E S W

MILES

Estes Park in the Days of the Trappers

High in the mountains of the Front Range in northern Colorado lies a small but beautiful valley known as Estes Park. A small village which graces the valley at the junction of the Big Thompson and Fall Rivers is also called Estes Park. The name of Estes Park originally meant the open valleys of the Big Thompson and its tributaries. However, when the tiny settlement grew sufficiently to be called a town, it became officially known as Estes Park, although a more common appellation is the Village.

Estes Park proper ranges in width from one to several miles and is approximately twelve miles long. It is actually a large open valley through which the Big Thompson twists and turns. The valley is not level and the gently rolling, green hills are dotted with small groves of trees and clumps of bright flowers. Today a small lake shines in the heart of the Park. It was built as a part of the Colorado-Big Thompson Reclamation Project, but its utilitarian purpose does not detract from its beauty. Surrounding the valley are snow capped mountains, the chief of which is Long's Peak. The Park is easily reached by scenic highways which carry the traveler through either the canyons of the Big Thompson or St. Vrain Rivers. Or if the traveler chooses, he may reach the Park from Grand Lake by way of the Trail Ridge Road which crosses the Continental Divide through the Rocky Mountain National Park.

This part of Colorado, which is today a splendid example of mountain beauty, was, in the days before recorded history, a great sea. The fossils embedded in the mud and sands which became rocks record the Age of Reptiles or the

11

Mesozoic Age which ended some 60,000,000 years ago. An uplift of land which formed the Rocky Mountains was responsible for the termination of this era. However, the Front Range grew so slowly that erosion caused the much older rocks to be exposed and these may be seen at the entrances to the Park. Volcanic action formed a hard core of rock but that, too, eventually eroded forming the present top of the Continental Divide which is called the Flattop Peneplain. It is along this peneplain that Trail Ridge Road crosses the Divide. The materials from this erosion spread out to the plains of the inter-mountain basins.

A new era began; it is known as the Cenozoic Age or Age of Mammals. The climate was warm, although in the Estes Park area it gradually became cooler and dryer, possibly because of more uplifts and volcanic action. While the land rose during this period, streams cut the raised plain surfaces and the mountains became more rugged. Erosion again proceeded to fill the inter-mountain basins and to build up the bordering plains. Toward the end of the Cenozoic Age, the area was again elevated and again the streams began to cut deep canyons.

The broad basin of Estes Park is due to a special type of erosion. The rocks in the valley were weak and great fractures running northwest, east-west, and northeast further weakened the area and caused the streams to flow through it. The Big Thompson and its five tributary streams—Fall River, Black Cañon Creek, Husted Run, Crocker Creek, and Fish Creek—were responsible for carving deep canyons through the basin. The period of glaciation, however, restored the level floor of the valley and, thus, the Park was formed for the men who were to come.

The Indians were quite familiar with Estes Park; the sites which have been discovered indicate that they lived in the broad, lower valleys and the gentle eastern and southern slopes of the Rocky Mountain National Park. The eastern boundary of the Rocky Mountain National Park is just a few miles west of the Village. In the two Parks there are still traces of old trails which are commonly called "Old Ute Trails." Since these have been traced westward from the mouth of the Big Thompson, it may indicate that the Indians who lived on the plains made regular excursions to the mountains to hunt. These Indians were, apparently, the ancestors of the modern Ute and Shoshone Indians. When later the Arapahoes came to the plains, they, too, made hunting trips into the Park. In fact, there is evidence that the Utes and Arapahoes fought over the hunting grounds for there is a battleground located at the west end of Beaver Park which shows the ruins of a fortified mound. However, after the entry of the white men into the Park there are no recorded accounts of Indian visits to the Park proper.

French trappers and explorers were among the first white men to visit northern Colorado. To these early visitors the most outstanding landmark in the region was Long's Peak which together with Mt. Meeker they named *"les deux oreilles"* or Two Ears. The trappers came into the Fort Collins area by way of the Platte River and hunted for furs. From this region the resemblance of the two mountains to two ears is quite striking. Other early visitors were the Spanish who explored along the base of the mountains looking for Indians, for the French, and for rumored mines. These Spanish expeditions influenced the area very little.

The first official expedition sent to northern Colorado by the United States government was that of Major S. H. Long. The Long party caught their first glimpse of the Rocky Mountains on June 30, 1820, at eight in the morning. Toward evening they could distinguish the range which was divided into three conic summits of about the same height; they assumed that one of these was the peak designated by Pike as the "Highest Peak" or, as it is now known, Pike's Peak. When Long and his men reached the base of the mountains, they camped near the mouth of the St. Vrain River where Fort St. Vrain was later built. Neither Long nor any of his party ventured into the mountains to climb the peak which was to bear his name.

In 1835 General Henry Dodge was sent on a military expedition of the Rocky Mountain region. One of his party was a Lieutenant Lancaster P. Lupton who realized the advantages of the fur trade in this area. He resigned from the

Army and returned to build one of the four adobe "forts" which were established on the South Platte between 1835 and 1838. The remains of Fort Lupton or Fort Lancaster, as it was sometimes called, may be see about one mile north of the present town of Fort Lupton. Another of these forts, from which the trappers went out into the mountains in search of furs, was built by Andrew Sublette and Louis Vasquez and was located about a mile south of the present town of Platteville. The third fort was Fort Jackson which was abandoned soon after its construction. Perhaps the most famous of the forts was Fort St. Vrain which was first known as Fort Lookout and then as Fort George. It was established in 1837-38; Marcellus St. Vrain, who was an employee of the Bent and Ceran St. Vrain Company, had charge of it for several years. It was located one and one-half miles below the mouth of the St. Vrain River and was abandoned before 1846. In 1859 and the early 1860's a settlement existed on the site of the old fort; it was here that Joel Estes was living when he discovered Estes Park.

Several famous travelers have left accounts of these forts. Among them were Dr. F. A. Wislizenus who came west in 1839, Francis Parkman who wrote *The California and Oregon Trail,* and John C. Fremont. Fremont made an expedition to the Rocky Mountains in 1842 to make a survey of the North Fork of the Platte River. However, he ascended the South Fork as far as Fort St. Vrain to determine the mouths of the Platte tributaries with the objective of ascertaining the advisability of building forts along the river. Fremont recorded that on July 9 they caught their first glimpse of the Rocky Mountains—Long's Peak. Fremont noted that he was pleased to see that among the traders and voyagers the name of Long's Peak had been adopted. The party stayed at Fort St. Vrain for only a day and then traveled north.

Rufus Sage is the only hunter who has left an account which indicates that he might have been in Estes Park although it seems likely that the Park was explored by other hunters and trappers before Sage. Sage lived at Fort Lancaster for two months; during this time he went on a hunting trip into the mountains alone. He followed a creek which headed at the base of Long's Peak. Continuing up the right hand branch, he then ascended the main chain of mountains to the left of Long's Peak. On September 30, he broke camp and traveled for ten or twelve miles through a "broad opening between two mountain ridges, bearing a northwesterly direction, to a large valley skirting a tributary of Thompson's Creek." Sage also described another valley four miles farther north which was watered by one of the main branches of Thompson's Creek. On a later trip in November he mentioned a large valley immured by lateral hills which was probably Moraine Park. Thus, it seems most likely that Sage did explore and hunt in Estes Park. Although other trappers were probably in the Park, there is no satisfactory evidence that they were nor is there any evidence that anyone settled in the Park before Joel Estes.

The two streams that have vitally affected the growth and development of the Estes Park area are the Big and Little Thompson Rivers. The naming of these rivers has been a matter of much speculation, and various stories have been advanced to explain the names. One such story is that the river which was called Thompson's Fork of the Platte (the present Big Thompson River) was named after a lieutenant in the band that Fremont led through the region. Fremont does mention a Thompson's Creek in his report and indicates it on his map made in 1842, but the list of men in the report does not include anyone by the name of Thompson.

Another version of the origin of the names is this one from the days of the California Gold Rush. A train of emigrants on their way west was joined by two men who drove a wagon pulled by two mules. These were brothers named Thompson; one was a giant, the other was small. When the party reached the banks of the present Big Thompson, the larger brother went out hunting only to return wounded by several Indian arrows. He died during the night and was buried on the banks of the stream. Thus, the stream received the name of the Big Thompson while its neighbor became the Little Thompson. As interesting

15

as this story is, it must remain in the realm of folklore since the California Gold Rush did not occur until 1849 and the stream and its name were recorded in 1842.

Several authorities credit the naming of the Thompson Rivers to David Thompson or his associates. According to these stories Thompson, a fur trader and explorer, was sent into the region in 1810 by the Northwest Fur Company, and he established camps on the Big and Little Thompson Rivers. These explorations are believed to have led him to Estes Park. However, the truth of the matter seems to be that Thompson was never in the area. It is true that he was sent west by the Northwest Fur Company to explore and establish trading posts, but according to his own narrative of his explorations he was never in Colorado. His principal explorations in the United States were centered around the Columbia River. It is, therefore, safe to assume that the name Thompson was not applied to the streams as a direct result of David Thompson's explorations of the northern Colorado region.

In the 1830's the St. Vrain area was visited a number of times by a trader named Philip Thompson who had a trading post at Brown's Hole. He sold mules to Sublette and Vasquez at their fort in the early '30's, and he was again reported in the region in 1839. Since he was a familiar figure in the St. Vrain region and a friend of the early traders, it seems possible and even probable that Thompson's Creek was named after him. From the name Thompson's Creek came the names of the Big and Little Thompson Rivers.

Millenniums of time and the hand of nature formed the Rocky Mountains, the river beds of the St. Vrain and Thompson Rivers, and the peaceful park lying high in the mountains. The land was seen by wandering Indian bands, then the region was discovered by courageous Spanish, French, and American explorers. The fur traders built their forts and robbed the mountains of their secrets. Yet still another phase of life was to come—the settlers. The first of these was Joel Estes.

16

Joel Estes

On October 15, 1859, Joel Estes stood on the summit of a plateau and saw for the first time the Park which was to be his home and was to bear his name.

Joel Estes was typical of the frontiersmen whose families had started the march across the country and who, in his turn, had moved his family west. His maternal grandparents, Germans named Hiatt, were among the first settlers in Kentucky. Peter Estes, his father, was a Virginia plantation owner of Scottish parentage who, despite his wealth in Virginia, moved to Kentucky. There he met and married Esther Hiatt, and their son, Joel, was born on the Kentucky frontier on May 25, 1806. When Joel was six, his father again moved the family to the frontier. It was in Clinton County, Missouri, that Joel grew to manhood. He was a big, gangling boy and not particularly handsome, but he met and married the pretty and fascinating Patsy Stollings. Patsy, whose real name was Martha, was born in West Virginia on July 6, 1806, the daughter of Jacob and Patsy Stollings. Joel and Patsy Estes, the true children of pioneers, were the first settlers to live in Estes Park.

Like most frontiersmen, Estes had many trades. He worked at odd times as a freighter from Liberty, Missouri, to the trading post of Joseph Roubideau which later became St. Joseph. At one time he ran an outfitting store, and he was also interested in gold prospecting. After he married Patsy on November 12, 1826, he moved his family to Andrews County, Missouri, and began the business that was to occupy most of his lifetime—that of stock raising and farming.

However, it was the search for gold and not the search

17

for new agricultural lands which brought Estes and his family to Colorado. It is not certain just when Joel Estes became interested in gold prospecting. Marshall Cook, a Colorado pioneer of 1858, was told by William Poe about a prospecting trip which Joel and Peter Estes were supposed to have made in 1833. According to this account, Joel and Peter Estes, William Poe, John Sollars, Joseph Gladden, Antoine Robidoux, and about seventy trappers and traders left Independence, Missouri, for New Mexico and the Rocky Mountains. Joel and Peter and some others worked placer mines near Santa Fe. Then they formed a company of some twenty-five miners, trappers, and hunters to prospect for gold. They spent the winter along the eastern edge of the Sierra Madre Mountains and Ute Creek. The next spring the party continued northward along the Rockies and they found paying dirt when they reached Vasquez Creek which is now known as Clear Creek. This gold was apparently not sufficient to interest them for very long because they wintered in the Black Hills. They mined there until driven back to Missouri by the Indian menace. Unfortunately this story cannot be accepted at face value. Estes was supposed to have been away from home from sometime in 1833 until sometime in 1835; yet his son, Newton Estes, was born on May 11, 1835.

Whether or not Joel Estes had been previously interested in gold, he was interested in the California Gold Rush. At that time he was the father of thirteen children—eight boys and five girls—who all grew to adulthood. In 1849 he left his family and with his oldest son, Hardin, crossed the plains and mountains to California. This western trail may not have been new to them for it is believed that they may have made one trip to the West prior to '49 and gone as far as Baker City, Utah. At any rate, in 1849 they prospected in Grass Valley, California. Here they struck a rich mine which they sold for $30,000. Thirty days after they sold the mine, it was resold for half a million dollars. Not too much is known about this California trip except that they must have had encounters with Indians for Hardin bore the marks of Indian arrows for the rest of his life.

18

Joel and Hardin Estes returned home, but, with the restlessness of their forefathers, they set out in 1855 for Oregon and California in search of a new home site. Estes saw no place that suited him and again they returned to Missouri. It may have been on this return trip that he stopped at Fort Laramie and heard talk of gold in the Pike's Peak country. Estes found the lure of gold still strong. and when the "fifty-niners" began to pour into Colorado, Estes, his wife, and six of their children were among them. The children who came to Colorado with their parents were Jasper, Milton, Francis Marion, Joel Jr., Sarah, and Mary Jane. The claim has been made that the two girls were the first unmarried white women to come to Colorado.

The family did not remain in the Denver area long, but went on to a site near Golden which Estes named Golden Gate. From Golden Gate the family moved to what was known as the Fort Lupton Bottom. This move was caused by the fact that Estes did not feel that the placer mines compared with those of California, and he decided to return to stock raising and farming. On the St. Vrain the family cut hay, put up log cabins, and settled down for a hard winter which turned out surprisingly mild.

Estes was popular with both white men and Indians. It was while he was living on the Fort Lupton Bottom that he became president of the first club to keep authentic records of land titles in Colorado. The formation of the club was occasioned by the frequent quarrels among the settlers regarding claims. The function of the club was to settle such disputes. Among the Indians he was known as the Big White Chief because of his large, rawboned physique. His son, Francis Marion, described his father as the William Penn of the West. "While other men battled for their lives with the Indians, my father was always on the best of terms with them, and he traveled across the plains without fear." However, if the story of the Indian encounters on the California trip is credited, it must be realized that his friendliness was not known everywhere.

It is regrettable that among his many talents Joel Estes was not a writer so that he could have left an account of his discovery of Estes Park. The accounts of the discovery differ widely, and it is impossible to determine accurately who accompanied Estes on his first trip to the Park. If all of the reports are credited, a larger number of people than would seem possible were there. Marion Estes, then a boy of about thirteen, claimed to have left Fort Lupton with his father to hunt in the mountains. While hunting they discovered and followed an Indian trail to the summit of a plateau that overlooked the Park on October 15, 1859.

Milton Estes, who was nineteen, declared later in his "Memoirs of Estes Park" that he and Joel traveled to the head of the Little Thompson Creek on a hunting and exploring trip. They thought at first that the Park was North Park, but they gave up the idea when they could discover no signs that white men had ever been there.

The account of the discovery of the Park given by Joel, Jr., differs from the others in several respects. The boy's youth—he was eleven—must be considered in determining the accuracy of the story. According to young Joel, he and his father returned to Missouri on business and to bring out more supplies and cattle in March, 1860. When they returned that summer, Joel, Sr., and a George Smith struck out prospecting and found the Park.

Two other men claim to have been in the party which first saw the Park. Dunham Wright, who later spent a winter with the future Senator Henry M. Teller and Joel Estes in the Park, claimed to have inspired the trip and to have accompanied Estes to the Park. Wright stated that in the late summer of 1860 he met an old trapper named Michael Jones who described a "little park at the foot of Long's Peak" to him. Wright became so interested that he joined Estes in an inspection tour of the Park. The other man who may have been there was David Hiatt of Fremont County, Iowa. His son, C. M. Hiatt, claims that his father was a member of the party that discovered Estes Park.

Estes did not move his family to the Park immediately although he saw the possibilities of stock raising there. Milton said that they built two houses and corrals and drove their stock up from the ranch in 1860. Apparently a party

20

spent the winters of 1860-61 and 1861-62 in the Park looking after the cattle. According to young Joel, the family did not move to the Park right away because of the Civil War. Estes decided to take his slaves east. These Negroes had been with the family for a number of years. He put them on a farm in Missouri and gave them livestock, provisions, and their freedom. He did not return to Colorado until 1863.

When Joel Estes had made sufficient preparations to move to the Park, there were two families—his own and his son Milton's. Milton had married Mary L. Fleming of St. Vrain on August 11, 1861, in the first wedding in that part of the country. Their third child, Charles F. Estes, was the first white child to be born in Estes Park. Unlike his father, Milton Estes has left us an interesting account of life in the Park in his "Memoirs of Estes Park." The Estes family lived in a little paradise unspoiled by human contact. There was no end of game since elk, deer, and mountain sheep lived there in abundance and fishing was considered excellent. Jasper, Marion, Milton, and Joel, Sr., were the hunters for the family and Joel, Jr., was the fisherman. The security of the family depended upon the hunters since the clothes they wore, the food they ate, and the cash in their pockets depended upon the wild animals. Their clothes were made from hides. Beaver was used for caps, elk for coats, antelope for shirts, and deer for pants, mocassins, and gloves. Their only cash commodities were the skins and hind quarters of deer, elk, and sheep which they took to Denver and sold for gold dust.

Life may have been ideal, but it was lonely since they were the only occupants of the Park. When the Byers party visited the Park in August, 1864, they were heartily welcomed for they were the first visitors in a year. The party composed of William N. Byers, editor of the *Daily Rocky Mountain News*, Professor Velie, Professor Parry, and George Nickols came to the Park because they wished to climb Long's Peak. They stayed with Estes and his family for two nights. They found the family most hospitable, and Byers described Mrs. Estes as a pleasant old lady of forty-five or fifty years.

Although the party failed in their attempt to climb the Peak, Byers returned to Denver to write an account of the trip. In this article, published in the *Daily Rocky Mountain News,* Byers named the Park in honor of his host. Thus the famous pleasure resort, a future which Byers predicted, received its name of Estes Park.

The Estes family named all the mountains and streams in the Park, but they were all renamed after the family left except for Sheep Rock and Muggins Gulch. Sheep Rock was so named because it was a favorite haunt of the mountain sheep which were common in the early days of Estes Park. The Gulch was named for George Hearst who was nick-named Muggins by a Dan Gant who had cattle in the Park. Muggins was the herder, and he built a cabin at the head of the Gulch to prevent the cattle from straying.

Joel Estes kept every Sunday in the Park except one. The family had lost track of time, but during the following week someone arrived and told them the day. Even after a stroke in later life, he was taken on a bed and carried into church. He was a member of the Primitive Baptist Church. The first sermon in the Park was preached by the Reverend Richardson of Denver in Estes' home. Richardson was on a camping trip with his wife and a party of five. There were seventeen people who gathered to hear this first sermon.

The winter of 1864-65 was a long, cold one. A two and a half foot snow fell in November and drifted. Since the snow stayed until spring, the winter was very hard on the cattle. Estes decided to leave the Park for a milder climate and a wider range for his cattle. He sold the Park for a yoke of oxen to Michael Hollinbeck and a man called "Buck." The Estes family left the Park on April 15, 1866.

Estes went first to Texas and then to Washington County, Arkansas. Later he returned to Colorado where he settled in Huerfano County and returned to the stock business. Joel Estes died at Farmington, New Mexico, on December 31, 1875, at the age of sixty-nine years. Patsy Estes went to live with their daughter, Sarah. She died in Thurman, Iowa, on August 6, 1882, when she was seventy-six.

Today none of the Estes family live in the Park, but

they have not been forgotten by the Park people. In 1925 it was proposed that the Estes cabin site be marked with a large granite boulder. The next year such a monument was erected by the Chamber of Commerce. The stone was taken from a hillside about a fourth of a mile from where it was used. It weighs about two tons and stands about seven feet high. It was left in its natural state and a bronze tablet was placed on it. The tablet reads:

> In memory of Joel Estes, discoverer, October 15, 1859, Pioneers, Patsy Estes, Sarah Estes, Molly Estes, Milton Estes, Joel Estes, F. M. Estes, J. W. Estes. Presented by the Chamber of Commerce and grandchildren, Milton Estes, Joel S. Estes, Edwin Estes, Mrs. C. H. Graham, Mrs. W. I. Myler, and Mrs. G. D. Taylor, Norma Ritters.

One name is missing from the tablet, that of Mary Jane Estes who also accompanied her family to the Park. This monument may be seen at the junction of the Fish Creek road with the North St. Vrain road. In the school of Estes Park is a picture of Joel and Patsy Estes. It was presented to the school in 1940 by a great-grandson and a great-granddaughter of Joel and Patsy.

Joel Estes and his family were the first to enjoy the pleasure of living in the Park, but others were to come. Among them was Griffith J. Evans whose home was to become the first shelter for tourists such as the picturesque Englishwoman, Isabella L. Bird. No history of Estes Park could be complete without her story.

An Englishwoman in Estes Park

When Joel Estes and his family left the Park in the spring of 1866, it was not long deserted. The location of the Park was no longer a secret and the people began to flock to it. Among the first to come were James Nugent and Griffith J. Evans.

James Nugent, known as Rocky Mountain Jim, was one of those early trappers and hunters who have made the pages of Colorado history bright and colorful. He was a man of wild and varying emotions, a man who when sober was a perfect gentleman and when drunk, a veritable ruffian. His later life was dominated by a hatred of bears for in 1871, while hunting in Middle Park, he had been attacked by a bear and horribly mauled. The right side of his handsome face was scarred beyond recognition and the sight of the right eye destroyed. His left arm was torn and mangled, and he lost his left thumb. It was a wonder he didn't die for the bear had also nearly scalped him, but he recovered to become unjustly the boogy man for distracted mothers with erring children. This was the man whose cabin virtually guarded the trail from Lyons which was then the only road to Estes Park. He was also the man who so interested Isabella Bird during her visit to the Park.

His neighbor, Griff Evans, was a little Welshman who lived in the old Estes log cabin on Fish Creek until it burned in 1876. Squatters had added rooms until when it came into the possession of Evans, it was fairly comfortable. Although Evans became the first hotel keeper in the Park, he and Jim were not very friendly to visitors in those early days. They were afraid that these visitors might be interested in the land which they wished to keep for themselves. It was not long, however, before Evans realized that he could make a more profitable living from providing lodging and food for strangers than he could from ranching and farming. Jim, a born hunter, never became fully reconciled to the change. This basic difference in the two men may be held indirectly responsible for Rocky Mountain Jim's violent and untimely death.

As early as 1871, Evans planned to build a cheap hotel to accommodate those who wanted a change of air, fresh trout, or restored health. The *Chicago Tribune* remarked that they thought it would be worth a dozen Saratogas to the invalid, especially delicate women and those troubled with lung complaints. Evans finally decided to build several cabins grouped around the ranch house rather than a hotel. These cabins contained only sleeping rooms and the guests ate and lived with the Evans family. The idea was a success from the beginning and the invalids and healthy alike came.

One of the first of the early visitors was Isabella L. Bird, a well-known author of the last century. She was an indomitable Englishwoman who allowed neither ill health nor other difficulties to interfere with her world travels. She left in her book, *A Lady's Life in the Rocky Mountains,* the most marvelous description of the beauties of the Park ever written. This book describes her experiences in Estes Park during the fall of 1873.

Isabella Lucy Bird was born October 15, 1831, in England. She was the eldest of two daughters of an Anglican clergyman. Her sister, Henrietta, to whom Isabella wrote the letters which became her books, was two years younger. Although Isabella was a frail child, her father taught her to ride almost in infancy. This early training was to stand her in good stead when in later years she rode oxen, horses, mules, and yaks in her travels around the world.

When Isabella was in her late teens, an operation was necessary. A large fibrous tumor was removed from her spine, but she continued to have long periods of suffering with her back the rest of her life. When her doctor urged a long sea voyage, she had her first opportunity to visit America. Her father gave her one hundred pounds and told her she could stay as long as she had money. Isabella was gone seven months and returned with ten pounds.

Her family always kept all of her letters. When she returned, she was urged to put them into literary form. She wrote all of her books, which were published by John Murray of London, from letters sent home during her travels.

In 1873, following a visit to the Sandwich Islands, she again sailed to America. According to her biographer, Anna M. Stoddart, she spent several months in a sanitorium in the Rocky Mountains. This "sanitorium" was Griff Evans' log cabin set in the loneliness of Estes Park. Miss Bird was delighted with the scenery of the Park and interested in the people, particularly Rocky Mountain Jim.

Rocky Mountain Jim was the first person that she met when she came to the Park since it was necessary for her to pass his cabin in Muggins Gulch in order to enter the Park. This cabin resembled a den more than a home. It was built of rough, black logs with a mud roof and covered with furs laid out to dry. Aroused by the barking of his dog, Jim came to the door. What a fearful sight he must have created. He was a broad, thickset man wearing old and delapidated clothing and he was armed with a knife in his belt and a revolver in his breast pocket. However, it was his face which fascinated Miss Bird. At one time, she later wrote, he must have been strikingly handsome with his large, grey-blue eyes, aquiline nose and strong mouth; but now due to the encounter with the bear, one side of his face was repulsive while the other might have been done in marble. He greeted her with the manner of a gentleman and was most gracious to her then and throughout her stay in the Park. They spent much time together for Jim acted as her guide, and she became his confidant.

Miss Bird believed that Rocky Mountain Jim was one of the famous scouts of the Plains and because of some past crimes, he was forced to occupy a squatter's cabin and trap in the mountains. Jim also told her of his family. His father was a British officer stationed at Montreal, and his people were from a good, old Irish family. Jim had been an ungovernable boy, and he had fallen in love with a young girl he saw in church. His mother opposed his wishes, and he took to drink to spite her. When the girl died, Jim, who was eighteen, ran away from home to join the Hudson's Bay Company. When he was about twenty-seven he became an Indian scout in the pay of the United States government. It was while he was a scout that he was supposed to have distinguished himself by daring deeds and bloody crimes. He took up a homestead in Missouri, and he might have belonged to a band of border ruffians who terrorized Kansas during the Civil War. Then he came to Colorado. When Miss Bird knew him, Jim had a squatter's claim, forty head of cattle, and was a successful trapper. Whenever he had money he went to Denver and spent it in the "wildest dissipation." However, it is possible that James Nugent's romantic history was invented to impress the wide-eyed Englishwoman since on other occasions he claimed that he was a southern gentleman, the nephew of General Beauregard. In fact, the truth seems to be that he was a Yankee, born in Concord, New Hampshire.

After leaving Muggins Gulch, Miss Bird's party caught their first glimpse of Estes Park as it lay bathed by the late afternoon sun. As Miss Bird described it, "the rushing river was blood-red, Long's Peak was aflame, the glory of the glowing heaven was given back from earth."* Descending into the valley they came upon a small lake with a trim looking log cabin close to it. It was surrounded by four smaller cabins and two corrals. When Griff Evans ran out to greet them, she recognized a countryman. She was welcomed by the Evans' family in the large living room of the cabin— a room dominated by a large stone fireplace around which settlers and visitors gathered in the evenings. Evans assured her that he could take her in. To her joy, she received a cabin to herself instead of the shakedown she had expected. To be sure the cabin already had a tenant, a skunk under the floor, but if strictest privacy were accorded to each

*Isabella L. Bird, *A Lady's Life in the Rocky Mountains* (3rd ed: London: John Murray, 1880), p. 94.

roommate, none would be the worse for the close quarters.

Griffith Evans was half hunter and half stockman. He was a little man with a ready wit and was well-liked by many. He was fond of his liquor and although he had fifty head of horses and a number of head of cattle, he was always in debt. There were those who mistrusted him, however, for he had been raised to believe in class. He was always ready to bow and call someone "my lord." For this reason he was popular with the Englishmen who came to hunt in the Park but not with the settlers who came to live.

Life was simple and pleasant in the Park. Miss Bird reported that her day began at seven with breakfast. She ate with the regular household which consisted of Evans, his partner, Edwards, their families, and numerous guests. After that, small chores were done until noon. After dinner she generally rode with the others or helped Evans with the cattle. After supper they played euchre or mended. There were always strange prospectors and hunters who joined them in the evenings. Evans steadfastly refused to help these men in their search either for mines or game since it would jeopardize his monopoly of the Park. These gatherings represented true democracy to Miss Bird since such varying classes of society were represented.

The long evenings afforded Miss Bird time to record her impressions of the Park in letters to her sister. She described the Park to Henrietta making a comparison of it with their native England. To an Englishman, Estes Park suggests park palings, a lodge, deer, and a Queen Anne mansion. Estes Park combines all the beauties of the Rocky Mountain parks, but the Englishman must dismiss his ideas of an English park in order to accept the grandeur of Estes Park. For park palings there are mountains, for a lodge there are two sentinel peaks of granite guarding the only feasible entrance, and for a Queen Anne mansion, an unchinked log cabin. Miss Bird described the Park as having an irregular shape about eighteen miles long and two miles wide. Through this grassy glade the Big Thompson twists and turns. The sun is hot during the day, but the nights are near freezing. During the winter the Park is never snowed in, and the cattle can winter out of doors on the cured grass. The growing season is short and grains cannot ripen; but the wild flowers and trees flourish, making it a veritable garden.

On one occasion Miss Bird expressed the desire to climb Long's Peak so Rocky Mountain Jim agreed to guide her. Also in the party were Platt Rogers, later mayor of Denver, and S. S. Downer of Boulder who was later a judge. The climb was hard and Miss Bird said that she would not have accomplished it if Jim had not been determined that she should, and he literally pulled her to the top. The young men were not particularly impressed with their companion but when Rogers read her book later, he wrote this about her:

> Her physical unattractiveness which so influenced us when we first met her, was really more than compensated for by a fluent and graphic pen, which made the mountains as romantic and as beautiful as doubtless were her own thoughts.

Miss Bird left the Park on October 20 to begin a long trip by horseback. This ride was to take her as far south as Colorado Springs and across the Continental Divide. Many of her days were spent traveling in severe snow storms through new territory, quite a trip for a frail Englishwoman to take alone!

Failing to obtain money on her way back due to the Panic of '73, she was forced to return to the Park. But as she said, "It did not seem like such a hard fate." She arrived in the Park exactly one month and many miles after she had begun her trip. Everyone had left the Park except Rocky Mountain Jim and two young men who were to look after Evans' stock. She kept house for the two young men until her departure in December.

It was not long before their provisions became short. By rationing themselves to two meals a day and eating the elk that the men had killed to sell in Denver, they managed to live for about six weeks fairly comfortably. Finally Miss Bird decided that she must leave for although Evans had expected to return, he did not and the men were anxious

29

to start hunting again. Rocky Mountain Jim rode down to the plains with her. When they arrived at St. Louis which is now part of Loveland, they discovered a dance in progress. The settlers were much surprised to find that the quiet refined gentleman with Miss Bird was the notorious Rocky Mountain Jim whose name they had used to frighten their children. From St. Louis Miss Bird was to take the stage to Greeley where she could board the train. So it was at St. Louis that Isabella Bird, with many admonitions to give up the wild way of life, said good-by to Mountain Jim although they were to have yet another parting.

Some six months after the departure of Miss Bird, Griff Evans shot Rocky Mountain Jim. Probably the exact reason for the attack will never be known although there had been bad blood between them for some time. Five different versions were written to Miss Bird. Any one of these reasons may have caused the tragedy: Jim may have threatened Evans in a drinking spree; he may have insulted some of Evans' family; or he may have taken a stand against the land steal since the Earl of Dunraven was attempting to gain control of the Park at this time and Evans was helping him. Evans said that he shot Jim for insulting his daughter; there was also a claim that there was a woman in the case and that she was one to whom both men were paying attention. The most reasonable supposition, in the light of Jim's beliefs and Evans' actions, is that Evans shot Jim because Jim was standing in the way of complete control of the Park by the Englishmen. Jim's cabin was in such an advantageous place that he virtually controlled the entrance to the Park.

Jim apparently had gotten into the habit of telling Evans that he would shoot him some fine morning and then of hanging around Evans' cabin armed with a gun. One morning late in June, Jim and a friend named Brown rode up to the cabin. When Evans appeared Jim dismounted from his horse and leisurely brought his gun to bear, apparently forgetting that Evans had something else to do besides waiting to be shot. Evans grabbed a gun and fired twice. He killed the horse and shot Jim in the head. Ac-

MY HOME IN THE ROCKY MOUNTAINS

From a sketch by Isabella Bird in A Lady's Life in the Rocky Mountains.
This is the Griff Evans home where Miss Bird lived in 1873.
Presumably part of it was Estes' old log cabin.

LORD DUNRAVEN
From McClure's magazine, *October, 1893.*
Courtesy of the Denver Public Library Western Collection.

ESTES PARK HOTEL

Photo by William H. Jackson.

Courtesy of State Historical Society of Colorado.

A BIT OF ESTES PARK
Photo by William H. Jackson.
Courtesy of State Historical Society of Colorado.

The Highlands.
Estes Park, Colorado.
J. M. Ferguson, R. P. P.

THE HIGHLANDS

Courtesy of the Denver Public Library Western Collection.

THE POST OFFICE AND JAMES RANCH
Photo by William H. Jackson.
Courtesy of State Historical Society of Colorado.

ELKHORN LODGE

Courtesy of the Denver Public Library Western Collection.

ESTES PARK AND CONTINENTAL DIVIDE
Courtesy of the Denver Public Library Western Collection.

cording to the account published by the *Rocky Mountain News,* Evans did not wait to see if Jim were dead but rode down to the Big Thompson Valley and gave himself up.

Dunraven and his friend, Dr. Kingsley, rushed out of the cabin and found that Jim was not dead. He had been shot with buckshot which did not seem to have penetrated far enough to kill him. He refused to be carried into the cabin, and they were forced to take him back to his shanty. Dr. Kingsley said that his condition was so serious that he couldn't possibly live, but he did for several months. In fact, he lived long enough to write an article for the Fort Collins paper stating that the recent so-called purchase of the Park was a fraud and that the Earl had ordered him shot to get him out of the way. He was taken down to the plains, and he finally died in Fort Collins in September. The cause of his death was never fully determined. He had apparently recovered from the effects of the shooting but some buckshot may have worked in and killed him, or he might have died from the effects of bad whisky and too much of it. There was even the wild rumor that the attending physician had been hired to hasten his demise.

There was a trial and Evans was acquitted. A Lord Hague who was a chief witness had been in the cabin when Jim and Brown had appeared. According to the story that Brown told one of the settlers, they were returning from a ride and stopped to water their horses near Evans' home. Evans and Lord Hague were in one of the cabins drinking when they heard them. Hague put a double-barreled shotgun into Evans' hands saying, "I want you to protect me." But by the time of the trial Brown had disappeared; he may have been paid to leave. Another friend of Jim's declared at the trial that Hague had said to Evans, "Give him another; he's not dead yet." Other supposedly disinterested parties claimed that Hague had said, "Look out, Evans, he's going to shoot."

Evidence was introduced to show that Jim disliked both Evans and Hague. So Evans was acquitted and, according to Dunraven, ". . . the verdict was to the effect that Evans was quite justified, and that it was a pity he had not done it

31

sooner." The question of whether Evans had committed a horrible crime or had been justified was one not settled by the historians of the day.

Isabella Bird and Rocky Mountain Jim had promised each other that, if permitted, after death the one taken would appear to the other. Isabella devoted a great deal of time to thinking about Jim and writing to him. His letters gave evidence of his continued steadiness and there can be little doubt that there was a strong bond of friendship, at least, between them. Then in July Miss Bird received word that Jim was dead, but contrary to this first report Jim lingered. Miss Bird was in Switzerland at the time. One morning, as she lay in bed, she saw Rocky Mountain· Jim in his trapper's dress in her room. He bowed low with customary courteousness and vanished. When the news arrived with the exact time of Jim's death, it coincided exactly with that of the vision.*

There were those, such as Evans, who claimed that Miss Bird and Jim were in love. Whether Miss Bird, who a number of years later married a Dr. Bishop, was in love with Rocky Mountain Jim will never be known. An educated Englishwoman, who despite her ill health was brave and courageous enough to become a world traveler, in love with a rough, dirty, drinking, swearing trapper? It could be possible because one has only to read the beautiful prose that flowed from her pen to realize the compassionate nature she had.

. This has become the folklore of Estes Park, the story to be told in the winter's evening by the busy settlers who were to come. As a preface to their story is the story of Windham Thomas, Earl of Dunraven, who attempted to establish a feudal domain in America.

---

*Anna M. Stoddart, *The Life of Isabella Bird* (London: John Murray, 1907), pp. 83-84.

The Feudal Lord of Estes Park

The Right Honorable Windham Thomas Wyndham-Quin, Fourth Earl of Dunraven and Mount Earl, dominated the lives and activities of the people of Estes Park for two decades. He attempted to establish a European feudal domain in Estes Park and to become an American lord. Were it not for the indignation and protest of the early settlers of northern Colorado, Estes Park might yet remain the private property of an Irish noble family.

Lord Dunraven, who was born in 1841, was one of the few Irish peers who could boast of purely Celtic origin. He traced his descent from the historic Olliel Olum who was a famous third century king of Ireland. Dunraven was educated at Christ College at Oxford and after that he became a lieutenant of the crack cavalry regiment, the First Life Guard. When he was twenty-six he became a war correspondent for the *London Daily Telegraph* during the Abyssian War. He shared a tent with Henry Stanley of Stanley and Livingstone fame who was reporting the war for the *New York Herald*. During the Franco-Prussian War of 1870-71, he was a special correspondent for one of the big London dailies. He reported the seige of Paris and is said to have shown exceptional courage. Later he saw something of the Carlist Rebellion and a war in Turkey which was probably the Russo-Turkish War. During these years his leisure time was spent hunting wild game in various parts of the world.

Dunraven was twice undersecretary of state for the colonies. In later years he was associated with the government of Ireland, and he was Chairman of the Irish Land Conferences which paved the way for the Irish Land Bill.

33

He was also president of the Irish Reform Association, and he initiated a movement known as "devolution," a scheme which was wrecked, however, by extremists. He earned membership in the Most Illustrious Order of St. Patrick. Dunraven's government career was further enhanced by the fact that he was the only person to witness both the signing of the Convention of Versailles which ended the Franco-Prussian War and the Treaty of Versailles in 1919.

Dunraven was also an author. His books ranged in subject matter from hunting, spiritualism, and navigation to finances in Ireland. Among them were *Canadian Nights, Hunting in the Yellowstone,* and *Past Times and Pastimes.* The latter book described some of his impressions and experiences in Estes Park.

Lord Dunraven married a daughter of Lord Charles Lennox Kerr. Lady Dunraven became a leader in Irish society and a close friend of Queen Mary. She was renowned for her hospitality to her husband's American friends either at Adare Manor, Dunraven Castle, Kenry House, or her town mansion in London.

The Earl of Dunraven took his title from Dunraven Castle in Glamorganshire, but his principal home was Adare Manor in the county Limerick. The grounds of the Manor contained many famous ruins such as the Black Abbey, Desmond Castle, and the White Abbey. The Black Abbey was founded in 1299 by the first Earl of Kildare for the redemption of Christian slaves from captivity. Desmond Castle was the home of the Fitzgeralds dating from the time of Henry II.

Dunraven was a man of courage and determination and his strong character might easily be read from his face. He was a handsome man with a broad forehead and rather hollow cheeks. He had a strong chin and he wore, perhaps to soften his face, a luxuriant mustache. Since he had a large inherited wealth, it was not surprising that he early embarked upon a career of travel and adventure. A mighty and dashing man was the Earl of Dunraven! It was small wonder that the ladies were charmed by him and since he was not above a glance at a pretty ankle, his sojourn in Estes

Park was touched by the faintest aura of romance and scandal.

In the early days, there were many titled Englishmen who came to Colorado to hunt. From them Dunraven learned that the hunting was truly exceptional on the western plains so in the summer of 1872, he started West. In Chicago he became acquainted with General Phil Sheridan who gave him a letter to the commanding officer at Fort McPherson on the Platte. At the Fort the officer allowed two of his most famous scouts, Texas Jack and Buffalo Bill, to accompany the Earl on his hunting trip. They hunted on the plains the rest of the summer and, according to Dunraven's own story of Estes Park called "A Colorado Sketch," he arrived in Denver at Christmas time. When he heard of the fine hunting in Estes Park, he was determined to go there despite the bad weather. His party spent a day or two buying supplies and then they took the train to the Longmont station. It was cold—15° or 20° below zero—but the next morning they loaded a wagon with stores and started on the tiresome trip to the Park. As early as 1880, according to Dunraven, it was no trouble to reach the Park since there were two good stage roads but in 1872 there were no roads, only a track covered by snow and slippery with ice. With dogged determination the group followed the trail which ran fifteen miles across the plains from Longmont and then entered the mountains through a bright red sandstone walled canyon. From there the trail followed the St. Vrain River and continued to wind around the mountains until it entered the long valley of Muggins Gulch. Then the trail ascended the valley at an easy gradient until it reached the summit from which Dunraven could see the Park at his feet.

The Earl of Dunraven and his friends, Sir William Cummings and the Earl of Fitzgerald, first set foot in Estes Park on December 27, 1872. Griff Evans welcomed them and made them comfortable in a log shanty near the ranch house. The cabin had two bedrooms and a fireplace for which they were grateful, but despite the cold weather they unpacked immediately and started out to hunt.

Dunraven found the hunting exceptionally fine. In fact, Estes Park was a hunter's paradise where elk, deer, and mountain sheep could be found in abundance. Dunraven found that in the winter and spring the Park swarmed with game and even in the summer it was necessary only to know where to look to find the animals. The climate also appealed to him since the winters were enjoyable with long spells of fine weather and only short storms. The springs and summers were hot but with cool breezes. How different the history of the Park might have been had not Dunraven become enchanted with its beauty, climate, and hunting.

However, hunting in Estes Park very nearly cost Dunraven his life. One July he and his party, which included a Dr. Kingsley, were out hunting when Dunraven roused a mountain lioness. He was alone, having been separated from the rest of the group, when he saw her about to spring on him from an overhanging rock. He had time for one quick shot before the lioness hit him. His ball had gotten her in the stomach but failed to stop her. She had Dunraven down and was about to grab his throat when Dr. Kingsley came rushing up. A shot from his gun brought her down. Dunraven rose, a bit flustered to be sure, but remarked, ". . . those mountain lions are blasted nasty things to meet when alone, you know."

Dunraven returned to the Park in 1873 and 1874. It was in 1874 that he decided to obtain the whole of Estes Park for his own. He wished to create a private hunting preserve for the exclusive use and pleasure of his friends and himself and to become in fact, if not in name, the Lord of Estes Park. During trips to Denver, Dunraven had become acquainted with Theodore Whyte who was also an enthusiastic hunter. He was invited to be a member of the Earl's party in 1873 and the following year he was employed as Dunraven's agent to acquire the Park for him. Conferences with Denver lawyers showed Whyte that it would be necessary to find men to file on all land on which there were streams or springs and then the whole Park could be controlled. The land was under the Homestead Law which allowed only one hundred sixty acres to each person. Men were hired to make dummy entries and money was used freely among public officials. A large number of ranch hands were brought to Denver to file on land with the agreement that they were to hand over their claims when they were proved up. This method of obtaining land proved to be very expensive but money was no object to Dunraven. The government was petitioned for subdivisions and a survey was ordered. By May, 1874, about four thousand acres were filed, and in June and July about one thousand acres more were filed. The names of the men to whom these homesteads were granted do not appear again in Estes Park history, making it safe to assume that this was one of the most gigantic land steals in the history of Colorado. In fact, Dunraven's men made no attempt to comply with the law in proving up on the land. Most of the cabins, which were a necessary part of the claim, were merely four logs laid in a square. Some land was obtained from bona fide settlers such as Evans who sold his claim to Dunraven. However, this land constituted only a small part of the ten thousand acres which the Earl came to control.

With so many people involved and so much money changing hands it was impossible to keep the scheme quiet. A man named Thorn who was camping in the Park for his health discovered the plan and wrote the Denver papers. Public indignation was immediately aroused and there was a storm of protest. The *Denver Tribune* published a scorching article which was virtually a call to arms to protect American rights. The author reported a conversation which he had with a wealthy Englishman in the Park:

"Yaas—we shall allow all the campers and tourists that are a mind to come to, to come in the park this year, you know. Next year, however, we propose to have all the cattle out, the blasted heifers, and shall reverse the park for our hunting and fishing, you know. Of course, we can't let common people come in then, you know, blast 'em."

I heard but could hardly realize the impudence and audacity of my noble associate. What! An English "Milord," to lay claim to all the most valuable land of Estes Park that he and a few of his foreign bobs and nabobs, Counts and no accounts might have a convenient place to hunt and fish.

The article predicted that if the land grabbers were permitted to continue, they would have possession of some 38,000 acres embracing all the parks, canyons, and gulches leading out or into the Park proper. Since the cat was out of the bag, Dunraven and his agents took the only step open to them—that of pre-emption. Five thousand acres were proved up under the pre-emption rights of the Homestead Act. Dunraven paid the government $1.25 per acre but the middleman was quite expensive; each acre of land cost him five dollars.

About this time Dunraven formed the Estes Park Company, Limited. Although some of the land patents were granted right away, others were held for investigation. When there was a hearing before the land commissioners, the corporation plea was innocent purchasers and the patents were granted. All the land was transferred from the names of the claimants to the company at once. Just how much land Dunraven actually acquired is difficult to determine. He claimed 15,000 acres which was the greater part of the accessible land in the Park. However most of this land was held without title since whole sections were fenced and claimed which had never been entered. He managed to control about 10,000 of these acres by sheer intimidation of all new settlers. This coming of actual settlers in the fall of 1874 and the spring of 1875 put a stop to the wholesale entry of land. The balance of the holdings of the Company were secured through the purchase of lands entered by settlers or by the Company employees who at least saw the land. Many of the early settlers did not take kindly to the coercive methods which were used to control the land and they formally contested Dunraven's claims. At times they were successful in taking land away from him so that when the Company sold its land in 1907, it had only 6,600 acres to sell.

For thirty-three years Dunraven regarded Estes Park as his personal domain, but that does not mean that the Park settlers regarded it as such. They were as determined

38

a group of pioneers as has ever been assembled in one region and through the years they gradually bent Dunraven and his company to their will. The private hunting preserve was one of the first of many clashes between the Lord and his quite independent subjects. Their hostility forced him to give up the idea of the preserve although he did not give up hunting in the Park. Dunraven did not reside continously in Estes Park, but each year until the late 1880's he was a visitor. He brought large parties of relatives and friends with him to enjoy the hunting. One of his favorite spots was north of Estes Park proper on the North Fork of the Big Thompson where the wild country afforded good hunting. He had a lodge built in a small park known as Dunraven Glade. The ranch hands would bring supplies to the cabin which would then serve as a base of operations for hunting over the entire area.

In 1874 Dunraven decided to build a cottage for himself and a hotel for his friends. Albert Bierstadt, the famous painter and friend of Dunraven's, picked the sites for both the cottage and hotel with an eye to the best possible view of the Park and Long's Peak. Bierstadt, whose paintings hang in the Capitol in Washington, was so enchanted with the majesty of the Peak that he painted a picture of it for Dunraven.

The cottage and hotel were white frame; the cottage still stands beside Fish Creek facing the grassy, rolling Park. It is now part of the Camp Fire Girls' Camp Dunraven. The hotel, which was the first real tourist hotel in the Park, was built a few hundred yards south of the cottage. It was called the Estes Park or English Hotel and was elaborately furnished for those days, as was also the cottage. The hotel was often the scene of many large gatherings of famous notables.

However, Dunraven had trouble keeping a manager for his hotel. A succession of them came and went since Dunraven was not a particularly satisfactory employer and since the hotel was the headquarters for large groups of Dunraven's friends. Wild and riotous parties were the rule and not the exception at the English Hotel. Old timers told of the parties held at the hotel and how employees and guests alike would retreat to the ranch house for a little peace and quiet. One new manager was not sympathetic to Dunraven and his high jinks. Although Lady Dunraven had come with her husband to the Park occasionally, she was not always her husband's companion. So when Dunraven and his inamorata arrived and proceeded to enliven things, the manager protested as did the guests. Finally out of consideration for the guests, the manager proceeded to eject the Earl from his own hotel!

Dunraven was a thoughtful host to the friends he entertained in the Park. For their pleasure great quantities of whisky and other liquors were brought into the Park by the wagon load. If the liquor was not consumed during the season, trusty servants buried it until the next summer. One summer the Earl returned and could not find the liquor. He never found out whether the servants drank it or whether they failed to mark the correct location, but for years the favorite pastime of the settlers was to hunt for that whisky.

Theodore Whyte was probably better known to the Park settlers than was Dunraven. He had been responsible for acquiring the land for Dunraven, and he became general manager of the Estes Park Company. Whyte came to the Park with all the paraphernalia of an English gentleman. He rode most of the time with his men, and they never failed to use a gate as a hurdle. The settlers, naturally, were quite contemptuous of all this show until they learned that he did it to keep all hands in condition. Later they admitted that Whyte was a good neighbor if both the settlers and Whyte made allowance for differences in backgrounds and faults.

When the hunting preserve idea failed, the Company began to raise cattle in the area. Estes Park, however, did not furnish sufficient grazing land and the settlers confined the Company by surrounding it with their homesteads. The cattle were grazed on the North Fork range for several years, but the stock business could not pay expenses. In fact, the Company never did pay a dividend. In 1878 there were roughly 1,400 cattle in the Estes Park area. Considering the vegetation in the region, the grass must have been overgrazed. The cattle were branded with a cross and a bat (X) on the right hip, and they were described in various mortgages as "half breed" American cattle. Finally Whyte was told that the place would have to be self-supporting and the establishment toned down. He tried all means possible to keep the lands intact, but eventually he failed.

Whyte tried to force the settlers out so that the Company would have more land. His men cut fences and drove their cattle over the claims. Settlers continued to encroach upon lands that had been fenced by the Earl but did not belong to him. Finally land was homesteaded in the heart of the Earl's property almost directly in front of the English Hotel. This drove Whyte to more desperate measures. He threatened to fence Company lands so that the settlers could not reach their claims. A petition was laid before the County Commissioners asking for the location of roads to all parts of the Park. Whyte consulted with the County Attorney and was informed that the roads could be made legal highways and would have to be fenced or left open to the public. Whyte then offered the settlers roads if they would allow closed gates to be placed where the roads entered and left Company property. The solution suited the settlers and after that, the Park people and Whyte began to live together peacefully.

Dunraven became quite disillusioned about his Estes Park venture, and he left the Park in disgust in the late 1880's. He returned to the United States in 1893 and 1895 when he unsuccessfully attempted to win the America's Yachting Cup. After his failure he never returned to the United States. He lost control of much of the land in the Park, losing between $200,000 and $300,000 in the venture. Interest in the Park began to wane. A lake which had been formed by damming Fish Creek in front of the hotel was allowed to flow away. The hotel became run down, and eventually it burned late in the summer of 1911.

Whyte quarreled with Dunraven before he left the Park but Dunraven leased the property to him. Whyte, his wife, and daughters lived in the Earl's cottage until the late 1890's. Whyte was married twice. The first Mrs. Whyte was a Miss Webster who came to the Estes Park Hotel with her mother for her health. They were married in 1878, but she lived only a few years. After the death of his first wife, Whyte married Lady Maude Ogilvy, sister of Lord Ogilvy who had a ranch at Greeley. In 1896 Whyte and his family left America for England where Whyte managed a large estate until his death.

Dunraven sold his property in Estes Park to B. D. Sanborn and F. O. Stanley in 1907. The plans of these men were as different from those of Dunraven as night is from day. Dunraven's feudal domain was transformed by these two brilliant businessmen into a mecca for lovers of scenic beauty in America.

The Earl of Dunraven died in London in June, 1926. Today in Estes Park the mention of his name provokes mild interest, but in yesteryear it was a different story. Time has mellowed the memory of the Lord of Estes Park.

The Early Settlers of Estes Park

In 1875 the men who were to make their permanent homes in Estes Park began to arrive with their families. The history of these early settlers is not the story of one man nor one family but of many men and many families. This is the story of the people who created the Estes Park of today.

One of the early Estes Park pioneers was William E. James. James, who was born in Camden, New York, married Ella McCabe in 1865. He was in the grocery business when the Panic of '73 ruined him, and like many men, he came West. It was while he was in Denver that he and some friends came to the Park on a hunting trip. James was delighted with the Park, and he was determined to move there. The next spring, on May 4, 1875, he returned to the Park with his family. The family built their first cabin near what is still known as McCreery Spring. It was a simple one-room cabin with a lean-to kitchen. It was chinked inside and out, and the floor was of rough boards. The roof, however, was made of dirt which turned into a sea of mud when it rained or snowed.

Not long after, James found a more suitable location and the family moved to a new home site near Alexander Q. MacGregor's homestead on Black Cañon Creek. A friend had left James a small legacy which enabled him to buy his first herd of cattle, and he settled on bottom land where he could raise feed for the stock. However, it was not long before James found that he was engaged in a contest for eighty acres of his best land. He then realized that even if he won, he was cut off from public grazing lands by high timbered mountains to the west and private lands to the east. Since he felt that he needed more land, he again began to look for a new location. He found that there was vacant land on the Fall River west of Dunraven's property. To the west of this land, there was public land which could be used for grazing; therefore, in April, 1877, the James family moved to the present site of the Elkhorn Lodge.

Hardly were they settled in their new home when a hoard of tourists began to descend upon them. Most tourists failed to provide for their own food or camping equipment, and the Park ranchers were forced to look after them. Little by little the Jameses added facilities for caring for the summer visitors and thus, from these humble beginnings, one of the largest hotels in the Park was built. This was the Elkhorn Lodge which is still operating today. The Jameses were ideal hosts. James had a round, cheerful face, a happy manner, and the ability to make people feel at home. Mrs. James was held in high regard and much of the popularity of the Lodge was due to her personality. When James died in 1895, Mrs. James continued to manage the Lodge with the help of her children, Dr. Homer E. James, Howard P. James, and Mrs. Eleanor Estes James Hondius.

Dr. Homer E. James was one of the first to receive a degree in medicine from the University of Colorado. He practiced for a time; in fact, at one time he was the only physician in the Park. When his father died, he withdrew from practice to help manage the Lodge. However, he did not stay with the Lodge long and upon the death of his mother, Howard James and Mrs. Hondius became sole heirs by settlement with the other legatees. Then in 1939 the Howard P. James estate became the owner of the Lodge.

The James family was among the first of the families who arrived in 1875. Among the other settlers who came in 1875 were the Rowes, Hupps, Fergusons, and the Spragues. The year 1875 might be said to mark the beginning of permanent settlement in the Park.

In the fall of 1875, Israel Rowe, his wife, and their two children, Charles Judson, five, and Dora, two, moved to Estes Park. Rowe was employed as assistant foreman on the toll road which A. Q. MacGregor was building into the

Park, and Mrs. Rowe cooked for the road workers. When the road was completed, Rowe moved his family to a log cabin near MacGregor's ranch. Later they moved to a small cabin in front of the site of the present Stanley Hotel.

Rowe supported his family with his rifle. Game was killed and taken to Denver which had practically no domestic meat at this time. Generally the only fresh meat was the wild game brought in by the hunters. The hunters made several trips from the Park each winter; each trip took six days barring accidents. In Denver the meat was exchanged for staples. Rowe supplemented his income by serving as guide for the Englishmen in the region. He was thoroughly familiar with the entire area, and it was he who discovered the glacier which was for a time called Hallett's Glacier. It has now been renamed Rowe Glacier in honor of its true discoverer.

Rowe prospered while he was in the Park. He acquired land at the base of Mt. Olympus and built a nine room house. He grazed large herds of cattle on the ranch, but in 1882 he moved his family to Longmont so that the children might have better schooling. The ranch was sold and eventually became well-known as the Crocker Ranch.

Rowe continued to act as a guide in Wyoming and Colorado. It was in Wyoming that he contracted pneumonia and died. His daughter, Dora, married Ovid Webb in 1896, and they came to the Park to make it their home in 1909.

In 1870 Mr. and Mrs. Horace W. Ferguson and their family came to Colorado for Mrs. Ferguson's health. They joined the St. Louis colony at Evans where they first lived in a store building. That fall Ferguson bought a tract of land west of Evans and built a two story brick house for his family. However Mrs. Ferguson's health was no better so they moved to a farm west of Namaqua in the Big Thompson valley in April, 1873. In the winter of 1875 Ferguson went up to Estes Park to hunt. He decided it would be an ideal place to move his wife whose health was still poor. He took up a claim a half mile north of Mary's Lake. A cabin was soon built, and the family moved to the Park in April, 1875.

It was a wretched trip. Four days were required to

make the journey through ice and snow. Needless to say, the family was very happy to see their cabin even though it was no more elaborate than the usual Park cabin with the inevitable sod roof. It was in this cabin that the first wedding took place in the Park. Anna Ferguson was married to Richard Hubbell, a merchant in Longmont, in October, 1876.

The Fergusons discovered, as many Park settlers did, that Dunraven's Estes Park Company was an unfriendly neighbor. The Company ordered the Fergusons to move, claiming the entire place. However, investigation proved that the Company had entered most of the land in the name of a man who had never been in the Park. Their buildings were on public land and Ferguson filed for it. A piece of land had been left unfiled near Mary's Lake and a daughter, Mildred, filed on it. When title was secured to this property, the Company was persuaded to exchange lands.

In 1876 a Mr. Hill and a Mr. Beckwith built a sawmill just above where the overflow from Bierstadt Lake enters Mill Creek. They made all kinds of building materials and the following year the Fergusons obtained lumber from them. They put a shingled roof on their cabin and added four rooms. Then they began to follow the practice of their neighbors and keep boarders. They called their place The Highlands because Mr. Ferguson's people were from Scotland. In 1878 The Highlands was again enlarged by adding a large kitchen and a dining room to the main building. At that time five three-room cottages and five tent houses were used for rooms. Sixty people could be accommodated.

Eventually Mr. Ferguson bought eighty acres near Longmont and built a home there. His daughter, Sally, and her husband, Charles L. Reed, leased The Highlands and reopened it. Then in 1908 Reed and his brother-in-law, James Ferguson, bought holdings in Moraine Park, and in 1911 they built and operated the Brinwood Hotel.

Horace W. Ferguson was a native of Kentucky, but he spent his boyhood in Memphis, Tennessee. Then he moved to Missouri before coming to Colorado. His fame as a hotel man was exceeded only by his fame as a hunter for it was he who shot a brown bear on the shores of Bear Lake and gave the lake its name. Ferguson died in 1912 at the age of 86 years. His wife had preceded him in death in 1887.

Among the best known of the pioneer families was the MacGregor family. Alexander Quinter MacGregor was a lawyer in Milwaukee, Wisconsin, but in 1869 he came west to the Colorado Territory. For a few years he lived in Denver where he was clerk of the Arapahoe County Court, and then he took his bar examinations and was permitted to practice law.

As so many of the Park settlers had done he came to Estes Park first on a hunting trip. During that same summer of 1872, Clara Maria Heeney, a student at the University of Wisconsin, came to the Park with a sketching group conducted by H. C. Ford of Chicago. Her mother, Mrs. Georgianna Heeney, chaperoned the party. The next year MacGregor returned to Estes Park with Miss Heeney as his bride.

A. Q. MacGregor began his active life in the Park by constructing a toll road. The only road into the Park at that time was in very poor condition, and he saw that it would be years before a satisfactory county road could be built. Having some money to invest, he decided to build a toll road. By a grant of the territorial legislature, he was given exclusive right to build and maintain a road between Glenn Evans, a few miles from Lyons, and Estes Park; he was allowed to collect toll on this road for ten years. MacGregor formed the Estes Park Wagon Road Company to build the road on March 10, 1875, with Henry Jensen, his mother-in-law, and himself as trustees.

Work had already been started on the road the previous fall and it was carried on during the winter. By the next summer the road was completed and was formally opened on Wednesday, July 28, 1875, at noon. Alonzo Parsons was the first gate keeper; he collected $31.95 for the first three and a half days the road was open. The charge was a dollar a team each way, but rates of fifty or sixty cents were given to those who used the road regularly. However, despite the fact that this was the first good road that the Park had ever had, the road was plagued with difficulties from the very

47

beginning. Some of the troubles were natural, such as heavy stones which ruined the roadbed, but others were man-made. A toll road was exceedingly unpopular with the people of the Park so fences were torn down or cut regularly. Finally the road was offered for sale and a group of Longmont businessmen bought it.

The MacGregors homesteaded on Black Cañon Creek on a slope facing Long's Peak. This was a corner of the Park which had been missed by the English company and which was suitable for stock raising. The family, consisting of Mr. and Mrs. MacGregor, their son, George, and Mrs. Heeney, moved into their claim cabin during the last of February, 1875. Mrs. Heeney also acquired land by using the pre-emption rights under the Homestead Act. Her property extended southward to include the land where the Stanley Hotel is now located, but in 1876 she exchanged this tract with the Estes Park Company for land lying along Black Cañon in order to keep their land unified.

The first post office in Estes Park was established June 2, 1876, and Mrs. MacGregor became the first postmistress. A small cabin on the hillside north of Black Cañon Creek housed the post office. The post office was a bone of contention for some years; the Englishmen wanted control of it but the settlers wanted it to stay at the MacGregor's. However, to all intents and purposes the Englishmen won when, in 1877, Mrs. Griff Evans was appointed postmistress.

MacGregor had many different interests in the Park. He may be said to have kept the first store for he supplied the settlers with a few necessities such as flour, cornmeal, sugar, salt, and butter. He also built a small sawmill which was operated from the flow on Black Cañon Creek. Since cash money was scarce he took his pay in the form of logs which the settlers brought in to be sawed. He did not neglect the tourist trade either. An early newspaper article listed two hotels in the Park, Estes Park House and MacGregor House. Board was seven dollars per week which included room and washing. Horses were taken care of for fifty cents per day if the owner fed them. Tourists who wished to build their own cabins were given long term leases. Eventually, however, the MacGregors withdrew from all these pursuits and devoted themselves to ranching although MacGregor continued his law practice and was associated with a Denver law firm. In 1882 he was appointed and then elected County Judge of Larimer County, and during those years the ranch was leased and the family resided in Fort Collins.

In June, 1896, when MacGregor and his son, George, were on a prospecting trip, MacGregor was struck by lightning and killed. He left three sons, George, Delbert, and Donald. Donald secured the interests of the other heirs and his family is residing on the home ranch now.

Another early settler was John T. Cleave who was born in Cornwall, England, in March, 1840, and died in Colorado on December 28, 1925. Much of his life was spent in Estes Park. He learned the carpenter trade before he came to America. It is not certain just why he came though possibly it was to answer the call for carpenters to rebuild the city of Chicago after the fire of 1871. His daughter, Mrs. John Griffith, said that he was engaged in the shipbuilding trade when he came west. At any rate, in 1874 Cleave was in Estes Park where he helped to plan and build the Estes Park Hotel for Dunraven.

Then Cleave homesteaded for himself and not for the English company as many men were doing. His claim was on Fish Creek about a mile southeast of the Hotel; there he built a home, store, and a post office. He was postmaster for many years. In 1877 an exchange of land was made with the Estes Park Company. Cleave received for his homestead one hundred and sixty acres at the junction of the Fall River with the Big Thompson. The reason for this change, according to one story, was that the joyful parties at the Hotel kept Cleave awake and when he protested loudly to Dunraven, the Earl persuaded him to trade lands. Thus all objections were removed to the hilarious parties. Later circumstances proved that it was a most advantageous trade for Cleave.

Cleave put up a building near the site of the present Hupp Hotel which served the family — he had married

Margaret May in 1882 or 1883 and they had two children, Paul and Virginia—as a home, store, and a post office. It appears that later he built a separate house.

The village of Estes Park sprang up around the new Cleave home. Mrs. Cleave began to keep summer boarders and the tourists began to recognize Cleave by his two favorite sayings, "Tell it to I" and "Bless m' Soul, young fellow." Cleave was a personage, a man around whom things revolved. He was a busy man who took an active part in community affairs; he was on the school board and was a vestryman at the Sunday services. After having lived happily in the Park for a number of years and having served the community faithfully as postmaster, he suddenly sold his property and left the Park.

For two decades Cleave had sold none of his land, but he had granted permission to those who wished to erect buildings on his property. In 1905 he sold his entire holdings to C. H. Bond and the Estes Park Town Company. Cleave and his wife moved to Fort Collins for they couldn't stand to see "the danged place overrun by tenderfeet tourists." From Fort Collins they moved to Mancos, Colorado, where they farmed, but in 1917 they couldn't stand to be away from the Park any longer and they returned to spend their last days. Mrs. Cleave died in 1921, and her husband died in 1925. They are buried on the John Griffith ranch.

Henry or Hank Farrar, a familiar figure to the old-timers, was one of the first guides in the Park. He built the first house within the present city limits of Estes Park. It was a simple one-room log cabin. Theodore Whyte, as manager of the Estes Park Company, ordered him off the land but Farrar replied that he knew the name used by the Company to file on the land and since the law hadn't been followed, he rather doubted if the Company would care to continue the matter. However, it was perfectly all right with him if the Company went ahead and paid the taxes since he was only interested in a place to live. Stalemated, the Estes Park Company deeded him forty acres on their west line and he moved his cabin. He was in the cattle business for some time before he moved to Wyoming. Eventually he went to Middle Park where he died.

The Reverend Elkanah J. Lamb was a pioneer in four territories. His home near Long's Peak was the tenth built with his own hands. He was born on January 1, 1832, and he grew into a powerfully built man standing over six feet tall. His wife was also endowed with more than the usual stamina for she climbed Long's Peak to celebrate her seventieth birthday.

Lamb first came to Colorado in 1860 but he did not remain long for he was sent to the Nebraska Territory by the United Brethren Church. He and his family returned to Colorado in 1873 when Lamb was given charge of the missions in the St. Vrain Valley. Then in 1878 Lamb moved his family to a site near Long's Peak. They were almost 9,000 feet high and only three miles from timberline but, in Lamb's words, "This location would seem to indicate more tangible and swifter strides to heaven than small salaries, partly paid in promises and hubbard squashes."*

Carlyle Lamb, son of the Reverend Lamb, said that the original road to Long's Peak was cut through the timber in 1876, but the family stayed in the crude cabins only in the summer for the first two years. Their first cabin was twelve by fourteen feet and roofed with poles, brush, and earth. The Lambs lived on their land as squatters for thirteen years before they finally made application for homestead rights. The Lambs went into the dairy business, entertained tourists, and guided parties to the top of Long's Peak for five dollars per trip. Carlyle Lamb made his first ascent of the Peak in 1880 with his father, mother, and brother. He was a professional guide for twenty-two years and made one hundred and forty-six trips to the top of the Peak.

The Reverend Lamb went back into the ministry and traveled the Colorado District of Our Brethren Church as presiding elder for five years. From 1895 to 1908 he preached the year around in Estes Park. The church was the school

*E. J. Lamb, *Memories of the Past and Thoughts of the Future* (n.p.: Press of the United Brethren Publishing House, 1906), p. 165.

house, and the salary was dinner and a free will offering on his birthday. In the winter he had to arise at dawn to reach the church where he had twelve faithful followers; however, in the summer the tourists augmented his congregation.

In 1915 at the age of eighty-three, Estes Park's first minister died; his wife followed him in 1917. They are both buried at Fort Collins. During Lamb's last years he wrote two autobiographical books, *Memories of the Past and Thoughts of the Future* and *Miscellaneous Meditations*. These books provide most enjoyable reading for anyone interested in Park life.

In 1902 the Lamb homestead was sold to Enos A. Mills. Mills was born in Kansas in 1870 and came to Estes Park while he was still a lad. After purchasing the Lamb property, he built the famous Long's Peak Inn using growing trees for pillars. The Inn has survived several fires, the latest of which occurred in June, 1949, and it is operating today. Mills was a naturalist as well as a hotel man, and he wrote many books on nature lore. He also wrote a guide book to Estes Park. However, he is particularly remembered in Estes Park because he was largely responsible for the creation of the Rocky Mountain National Park.

In August, 1918, Mills married Esther A. Burnell, a homesteader on the Fall River Road, and they had one daughter. Mills was killed in an automobile accident in September, 1922.

John Hupp and his family from Otterville, Missouri, were among the first arrivals in the Park. They settled in their first cabin which was built near a spring on Beaver Flat in August, 1875. Theodore Whyte ordered them to move since a James Daly had filed on the land for the English company. Hupp moved to upper Beaver Creek where the land was better. Hupp died after a few years but the family remained in the Park.

One of Estes Park's most valuable historians, Abner E. Sprague, was a pioneer in the Park. In later years he found time to record some of his interesting experiences in the Park in his two manuscripts, "Estes-Rocky Mountain National Park" and "Reminiscences of a Pioneer." Sprague first visited the Park in 1868 and again in 1872 and 1874. Then in the spring of 1875 he returned to make it his home. Sprague was born March 28, 1850, in Illinois, one of three children of Mr. and Mrs. Thomas Sprague. When the family came to Colorado, they settled near Loveland. In the spring of 1875 a friend, Clarence Chubbock, and Sprague decided to homestead land in Estes Park. They found that Dunraven claimed most of the Park and that James, MacGregor, and Ferguson had virtually all the rest of it; therefore they made their claim in Moraine Park which was called Willow Park then. The young men then went back to Loveland for the spring round-up, expecting to return to the Park soon to build cabins. However, during the round-up Chubbock was shot and killed, and Sprague succeeded to his rights in the Park.

Sprague had the usual trouble with Whyte who ordered him to move but he refused. Herds of cattle, as many as two hundred head, were driven onto Willow Creek by Whyte's men who then salted them down on the meadows. The first time it happened, Sprague waited until the men were out of sight and then he sent his shepherd dog out. The dog took the herd down the trail over the moraine to Beaver Creek and they arrived ahead of Whyte and his men. The second time Sprague chased them to the Park and had a talk with Whyte. After that talk there wasn't a third time nor any further trouble with the Company.

Abner Sprague married Mary Alberta Morrison on December 20, 1888, at Hickman, Nebraska. He was a surveyor for the Missouri Pacific Railroad in Nebraska at the time, and later he was assistant civil engineer for the Union Pacific Railroad in Colorado. For three terms he held the office of county surveyor for Larimer County. Despite his occupation as a surveyor, his wife's and his first love was Estes Park and they were never long away from it.

Sprague's parents and his brother, Fred, and his sister, Arab, moved to the Park with him. They entertained tourists for the first time in 1876 and soon Sprague was operating the lodge which is known today as Stead's Ranch and

Lodge. He sold his interest in the Lodge in 1904 and left the Park for a time, but in 1910 the Spragues returned to build and manage Sprague's Lodge. The Spragues had no children but they claimed as their own Mrs. Sprague's sister's children, Edgar Stopher and Alberta Stopher Miller. Edgar Stopher manages the Lodge now.

When the Spragues retired, they moved to the Village where they built a home. During the winter of 1943 they had planned to live in Denver at the Brown Palace Hotel. They had been in Denver less than a week when Mr. Sprague was taken ill. After a two-day illness, he died December 27, 1943, at Presbyterian Hospital in Denver.

Among the other early settlers was William T. Parke. He owned a photography business. He also owned one of the first general stores in the Park which he sold to Samuel Service. Service, who was born on July 3, 1860, in Billyeaston, County Antrim, Ireland, came to the United States in 1863. Several years later he married Sadie Boyd in Sterling, Colorado, and in 1902 they planned a trip to Ireland but before leaving they came to Estes Park. They fell in love with it, postponed their trip, and settled in the Park. They sold a quarry and store which they owned in Lyons and bought W. T. Parke's grocery store. When the village of Estes Park was organized, Service purchased a lot on main street and maintained his business there until 1929. Service died in 1937. He was survived by his second wife, Mrs. Minnie Service.

Among the other men to play a part in early Estes Park life were Carl Piltz, H. P. Welcome, and Shep Husted. Carl Piltz came to the Park in 1902 and went into the blacksmith trade and then into stone masonry. Welcome was the only veteran of the Civil War of which the Park could boast. He was an early ranch owner who died about 1910. Shep Husted was a pioneer Estes Park guide. He came to the Park in 1888 and lived there until he died in 1942. Husted is particularly remembered for the numerous trips he made to the top of Long's Peak as a guide.

Artists early discovered the Park. Among them was Charles Partridge Adams who was a noted landscape artist.

54

He had a home in Moraine Park and he maintained a studio on Fish Creek in the early 1900's. Another artist to capture the beauty of the region was R. H. Tallent who moved to the Park in 1898 with his wife and two sons, William and Lee. Tallent died in 1934.

Other early day settlers included Milton Clauser, Jim Fuller, Warren Rutledge, John Manford, E. B. Andrews, John and George Adams, Pieter Hondius, A. Griffith, Mark Barthoff, and J. Frank Grubb.

The mortal remains of the early settlers are scattered among the cemeteries of the bordering plains and private graveyards on Park ranches because Estes Park does not have a cemetery. Estes Park is a vacation land and the early planners of the village did not wish to bring even a shadow of sorrow or grief into their beautiful Park so a cemetery was never planned.

The men and women whose lives have been briefly sketched in this chapter are by no means all of the people who lived in the Park. They are merely representative of those who enjoyed life in Estes Park and were eager to share their good fortune with those who came to enjoy the beauties of nature. Today Estes Park is no longer a pioneer park: it is a vacation resort for the nation. It was through the pioneer encouragement of the tourist trade that such a transition was possible. Before many people would come to the Park, however, new and better roads had to be built.

The Roads to Estes Park

When Joel Estes came to the Park, he followed a trail from the present site of Lyons, up the St. Vrain River, over the mountains to the Little Thompson River, through Muggins Gulch and over Park Hill. This was probably the trail that the trappers had used in very early times although there were three other trails to the Park. One came over Bald Mountain near Loveland and another came from Berthoud up the Little Thompson for twelve or fifteen miles and then went northwest up Bracket Gulch. From there the trail turned west for several miles over Elk Ridge to a point on the present North St. Vrain and then came into Estes Park. The last trail came from the south in the same direction as the South St. Vrain Road does today. However, despite these other trails, the path which Estes used came to be the most popular route.

When Estes was preparing to move his family to the Park, he had to transport all of his worldly goods on horseback. Later he improved the road so that a two-wheeled cart could be used, and by the time he left in 1866, careful driving could maneuver a four-wheeled conveyance along the road. It was years, however, before the trail could be called a road in any real sense.

After W. N. Byers made his laborious trip to the Park in 1864, he described the trail that he and his party had to follow. When they left the plains, they followed the St. Vrain which they found to be a beautiful but swift stream. They had to cross it seven times, and they found the first two crossings very deep. They hadn't been told that the river forked and they took the wrong fork and had to return.

When they did start up the north fork, they found the trail very dim and choked with a dense growth of weeds, grass, and vines. The first night they camped in a meadow of grass that was higher than the horses' backs. Then the next morning they left the St. Vrain and began climbing the mountains in earnest. Finally they reached a lofty ridge from which they made a steep, sliding descent to a valley and then ascended another ridge. When they came down that ridge, they reached the Little Thompson. After they crossed it they had to toil up another long steep hill. They had managed to bring a wagon that far, but now they were forced to leave it. Soon, however, the trail changed and they reached the head of the creek. When they climbed the last long, grassy divide, Estes Park lay before them, "a very gem of beauty."

Road improvements were made by Griff Evans and Rocky Mountain Jim when they moved to the Park. They cut brush along the creek bottoms and removed stones. Despite their work, the comments made by visitors were not very complimentary. Abner Sprague who used the road on his first trip to the Park called it a poor horse trail. Mrs. Hattie Carruthers, who described a trip overland by prairie schooner from Iowa to Estes Park in 1874, said the road was called a road only by courtesy. The rocks, streams, and steep ascents made any trip to the Park something of an adventure.

This was the condition of the road when Alexander Q. MacGregor obtained a grant from the territorial legislature to build and maintain a toll road into the Park. The new road, which was opened in July, 1875, followed the St. Vrain River. At that time there was no town of Lyons but the road came around the base of a huge sandstone rock called Steamboat Rock near the present town. For three miles it followed the North St. Vrain and then it turned right through an opening. It followed this defile up three miles to the mountain top and followed the mountain top west until it reached high summits. From there the road dropped into deep ravines until it reached a pretty valley called Musk Valley. From this valley the road climbed to a point from which the Platte River could be seen on the plains, and from there the road descended to the valley of the Little Thompson. Then it followed the same route as the present North St. Vrain road does today. The toll road could not follow the river exactly because of rocks, so today parts of the old road are visible on Moose Hill, in Moose Park, and Little Elk Park.

MacGregor formed two companies to aid in the construction and collection of tolls for his road. The first was the Estes Park Wagon Road Company which was formed March 10, 1875, and the second was the Estes Park Toll Road Company which was formed four years later. The trustees, which were MacGregor, his wife, and his mother-in-law, formed this company to build a short road to connect with the first toll road in the Park.

Various and sundry problems made MacGregor decide to sell his road some years later. It was purchased by a group of Longmont businessmen. The new owners made a serious mistake by immediately raising the toll charges. The Park settlers who had never approved of the toll road protested immediately and vigorously. The climax was reached when a John Walker and a Norman Billings attempted to pass the gate without paying. The owners had posted a man at the gate with orders to shoot to kill if the tolls were not paid. Walker and Billings paid. Then, however, the teamsters who used the road pulled the gate down. They were arrested and taken to Fort Collins where a justice ruled that the owners would have to prove the right to obstruct the road. The teamsters with Abner Sprague's help secured Denver lawyers to plead their case which went to the district court and then to the state supreme court. The owners were finally defeated, and by the turn of the century Estes Park had a free road.

Carlyle Lamb and his father, the Reverend E. J. Lamb. spent several weeks cutting a road to the foot of Long's Peak in the spring of 1876. It went past Lily Lake and much of the present highway follows this original road. Two years later the Lambs cut a pony trail to timber line on Long's Peak for the convenience of the mountain climbers. This trail was replaced in 1882 by a more carefully surveyed path. Lamb claimed that he had a charter to collect toll over his road that led to the house. The toll gate was at the south end near the house and the gate was left open so that visitors might go on up to the house. Since this was the end of the road, the visitor had to return the way he came. When he turned to leave, he would find the gate closed and one of the Lambs on duty. He was then asked to pay toll for both ways.

The original road from Loveland to Estes Park did not follow the Big Thompson canyon since a road through the Narrows was thought to be an impossibility. Loveland citizens contributed money and labor and with some county aid built the Bald Mountain County Road. Bald Mountain is seven or eight miles straight west of Loveland. The road followed a series of rough valleys and ridges several miles south of the Big Thompson through Rattlesnake Park and over Pole Hill. Eight or nine miles from Estes Park, the road crossed the divide at Diamond Spring. Then it made a swift and dangerous descent to the Park through Milligan Gulch, Solitude Gulch, and Emmons Gulch and emerged in the Park at the location of the present Crocker Ranch. The road was approximately forty miles long. It was always a free road, and it was used until after the turn of the century.

The present Big Thompson Road was not born in a slow process of evolution; it came into being as the result of plans and blueprints. C. H. Bond was responsible for convincing the county that a road could be built through the Narrows. He had served as sheriff for a term and during that time he had made many trips through the canyon. A petition inspired by Bond was laid before the county commissioners in September, 1902, asking for the road. The commissioners ordered the civil engineer to make a survey. When his favorable report was given, the contract was given to W. A. Riley. Riley was to build the entire Big Thompson Road, and the cost was estimated at $24,000. He was given a free hand to build the road as he chose.

The Big Thompson Canyon Road was completed in 1903, but in January, 1904, Riley made the claim that he owned the road. Riley asserted that the county commissioners and engineer had impeded rather than aided the road's construction, and that he was several thousand dollars short of the contract money. Bills had been allowed by the county and never paid, but despite the evidence of their bad faith, he had gone ahead and completed the road at his own expense.

The next week an announcement was made that an electric car line was to be built to the Park. A group of Loveland and Denver businessmen had formed the Loveland and Estes Park Railroad Company. The route that they planned to use was the road constructed by Riley, and Riley was appointed superintendent of the line. The county commissioners were, of necessity, spurred to action. They sent out workmen to take over the road but these men were successfully ordered off by Riley. Legal action was then taken, and a settlement was finally reached. The settlement, which was made in the fall of 1904, allowed Riley a little over eight thousand dollars. This made a total of $19,000 which he had been paid but this did not pay him for all of his expenses in building the road. Since Riley had settled with the county, the electric railroad line was never built. This was the closest Estes Park ever came to having a railroad for although two railroads, including the Union Pacific, had sent surveying parties to run lines through the Park in 1881, nothing ever came of their plans.

For several years after the Big Thompson Road was completed, only enough work was done to keep it passable. F. O. Stanley, the millionaire, offered to keep the road in good condition in exchange for the exclusive franchise to carry passengers over it. His offer was refused because of the monopoly it would grant. Until 1919 the road remained a one-way track, and then the county and state began the improvements which have made it one of the most scenic highways in northern Colorado.

When F. O. Stanley came to Estes Park, he became interested in developing the Park as a tourist resort. He immediately saw the necessity of better roads, possibly because he drove the first automobile into the Park. In the fall of

1906 he decided to find a better location for the road from Longmont to Estes Park, and he selected the route of the present North St. Vrain Road. Burlington Railroad officials promised to help finance the new road. It was definitely to their advantage to do so because they used Estes Park as an advertising lure for their railroad. A right-of-way was secured in February, 1907, and work was started a month later. However, the railroad does not seem to have paid their share of the cost, and Stanley was forced to bear the cost alone. He maintained the road a year before he turned it over to Boulder and Larimer counties.

Not all the roads to Estes Park come from the plains. Two roads have been built to connect Estes Park and Grand Lake. The first was the old Fall River Road which was built by the state in 1920. It was considered quite a marvel as a mountain road but, nevertheless, it had definite disadvantages. There were very dangerous curves and the snow kept it closed for all but two months of the year. When a new road was considered, the Bureau of Public Roads decided to follow the old Ute Trail over the mountains. Not only did this route prove more advantageous for construction and maintenance reasons but it was far more scenic. Views from the Fall River Road were confined largely to the Fall River valley while views from the new Trail Ridge Road varied from valleys and forests to rugged peaks. Trail Ridge Road was built in the early 1930's. It is remarkable for achieving the highest point to be reached on a through highway in the United States.

Public transportation from the rail lines on the plains was early available in the history of the Park. From 1878 to the early 1900's regular horse-drawn stage lines were maintained from Longmont to the Park. In 1905 a line was established over the new Big Thompson Road. It connected the Colorado and Southern Railroad at Loveland with the Park. The trip took all day but two years later an auto stage line commenced operations over the route and reduced the time to less than three hours. The Stanley Steamers invented by F. O. Stanley and his brother were used on the lines run from Loveland and Longmont to Estes Park. However, the auto stages must have lost some of the thrill of adventure connected with the horse-drawn stages. Abner Sprague described one trip that he made from Loveland to Estes Park in a stage coach. They were traveling along the canyon road and reached a place where the water was raging from wall to wall. He had to take a saddle horse and ride through the strong current to find the road bed so that the stage could proceed.

June 18, 1908, was a momentous day in the lives of the people of Estes Park. Claude Clauser who was a driver for one of the Lyons-Estes Park Auto Cars arrived with the mail at 1:15. This was four hours earlier than the mail generally arrived by stage. Arrangements were soon made for the mail to be carried regularly by auto. That morning Mr. Clauser had set another record by driving to Lyons in an hour and a half. By August, 1908, the Loveland-Estes Park Auto Company had been responsible for bringing four thousand passengers into the Park. This increase in tourist trade and comfort was quickly realized by the Park people. In 1906 the transportation company was using ten stage coaches, but in 1908 they were using ten Stanley Steamers.

Thus from the barely passable trail that Joel Estes used to reach the Park, roads have been developed which rank with the very best in construction and ease of travel.

ESTES PARK IN 1908
Courtesy of the Denver Public Library Western Collection.

F. O. STANLEY
Courtesy of Clatworthy Studios, Estes Park.

NEW STANLEY HOTEL

Courtesy of the Denver Public Library Western Collection.

ESTES PARK IN THE TWENTIES

Courtesy of the Denver Public Library Western Collection.

MT. MEEKER AND LONG'S PEAK
Courtesy of Matthews Studio, Estes Park.

BEAR LAKE AND LONG'S PEAK
Courtesy of Mathews Studio, Estes Park.

DREAM LAKE TRAIL
Courtesy of Matthews Studio, Estes Park.

ESTES PARK TODAY

Courtesy of Clatworthy Studios, Estes Park.

Tourists in Estes Park

The beauties of nature which are found in and near Estes Park have drawn people to the Park from all over the world. The Park proper is a long, irregularly shaped valley surrounded by lofty mountains and dominated by snow capped Long's Peak. The valley is covered with a carpet of grass and dotted with groves of trees and clumps of brightly colored flowers. The Big Thompson winds its shining way through the valley joined at intervals by rushing Fall River, somber Black Cañon Creek, lazy Fish Creek, and picturesquely named Husted Run and Crocker Creek. Near by are the descriptively named Horseshoe Park, Moraine Park, Hidden Valley, Black Cañon, Devil's Gulch, and the canyons of the Big Thompson and St. Vrain rivers. There is also the never-to-be-forgotten Trail Ridge Road which provides breathtaking views of both sides of the Continental Divide. Truly a vacation in Estes Park is very close to a vacation in paradise.

In the early days the men and women who lived in Estes Park chose the Park as their home because of its beauty, and they were not surprised that other people made the long, hard journey just for a vacation in the Park. These early settlers were soon occupied with caring for the visitors, and they were not reluctant to assume their new role as hosts. In the words of one settler, "Before the tourists came to Estes Park it was only a cattle ranch and not a good one at that."

One of the earliest known attractions of the Park was near-by Long's Peak which challenged many mountain climbers. Just who was the first white man to ascend the Peak is a disputed fact. The credit for the first climb is generally

63

given to the Major J. W. Powell party who climbed to the summit of Long's Peak in August, 1868. However, as early as September, 1860, *The Western Mountaineer,* a paper printed at Golden City, contained an article to the effect that a Mr. Cromer had climbed the Peak the previous week. The article stated that there were no evidences of "any person having visited the summit since the government party many years ago." The story was signed Sniktau which was the nom de plume of E. H. N. Patterson. The mention of a former government party having ascended the Peak weakens the story since there is no knowledge of such a party. However, Patterson's son defended the authenticity of this climb by asserting that his father was under the impression that Long's party had climbed the Peak.

E. W. Andree in his picturesquely named pamphlet, *Traveling in the Sunset Trail with an Ox Team to the Rocky Mountains,* claimed that he climbed Long's Peak in the summer of 1861. According to Andree, he and his friends, John Bartz and Joe Baer, left Black Hawk in July and a short time later climbed the Peak. Roger W. Toll, who was at one time superintendent of the Rocky Mountain National Park, did not feel that the claim was sufficiently substantiated by details of route, time, or landmarks. Toll believed that the party had climbed Arapahoe Peak.

There were others who attempted to climb the Peak and failed. Professors C. C. Parry and J. W. Velie, who were studying the physical features of the region, climbed Long's Peak in August, 1864, but they failed to reach the main summit. Parry and Velie were accompanied by William N. Byers, the editor of the *Rocky Mountain News,* and a George Nickols. The party ascended the northwest side of the Peak and camped on the night of August 19th at 11,000 feet. The next day they climbed the east peak which is Mt. Meeker and added their names to the five already there. The main peak to the west was still unclimbed when they descended.

The members of the Powell party which is generally given the credit of being the first to climb the Peak were* Major J. W. Powell, W. H. Powell, L. W. Keplinger, Samuel Garman, Ned E. Farrell, John C. Sumner, and W. N. Byers.

The group made Grand Lake their base of operations instead of Estes Park. They left Grand Lake on August 20, 1868, and on the 23rd they stood on the extreme summit of Long's Peak.

Byers described the summit as a nearly level surface of some five or six acres paved with irregular blocks of granite without vegetation except for a little grey lichen. From the top, nearly all of Colorado was visible. There was a bird's eye view of Denver, Pike's Peak, Middle Park, and the Platte and all its tributaries. The various ranges such as the Saguache, Gore, Elkhorn, Medicine Bow, Sweetwater, and the Sangre de Christo were distinguishable. Over thirty alpine lakes could be counted from the summit. Byers declared that the view was one of the finest in the world.

Since then, Long's Peak has been climbed by many and there are twenty different routes to the top. Although the majority of the climbers have been men, many women have enjoyed the thrill of the climb and the view. The first woman to climb Long's Peak was Anna E. Dickinson who was a famous lecturer and author. She accompanied the Hayden surveying party when they made an ascent of the Peak on September 13, 1873. This was the largest group to climb the Peak up to that time; the party included Professor F. V. Hayden, Miss Dickinson, her brother, the Reverend John Dickinson, Ralph Meeker, W. N. Byers, and several members of the Hayden expedition. The climb was comparatively uneventful until they reached new snow some three hundred yards from the summit and then traveling became slippery and dangerous. When they reached the top, it was so cold that they spent very little time on the summit before returning. At the bottom they discovered another party containing three women on its way up. Thus by a half day, Anna Dickinson earned the distinction of being the first woman to climb Long's Peak.

The next year a group of climbers found a cloak folded in a crevasse. They believed it belonged to Miss Dickinson. At any rate it was forwarded to her from Denver with the compliments of the finders.

A short time later, Rocky Mountain Jim led Miss Isabella Bird to the top of Long's Peak. According to her story of the ascent, Jim virtually pulled her to the summit. She would have gladly turned back, but Jim was determined that she should reach the top. Despite her fatigue and giddiness, she admitted that the view was well worth the time and danger.

Some of the early climbs were rather unusual. In August, 1880, George B. McFadden and six of the twelve members of the Longmont Cornet Band reached the top and played a special program of band music. The first moonlight climb was made by H. C. Rogers in August, 1896. Enos A. Mills made the first winter climb in February, 1903. The young and old alike have climbed the Peak successfully. Harriet Peters climbed when she was eight and in 1904 Professor S. A. Farrand, aged 74, and Ethel Husted, 10, climbed unassisted. In July, 1924, Abner Sprague celebrated the fiftieth anniversary of his first climb by walking from Sprague's Lodge to the top of Long's Peak and back. He was seventy-four years old. However, the oldest person to climb was William Butler of Longmont who made the climb when he was eighty-five. Perhaps the most unusual climb was made on June 14, 1927, by Lucille Goodman and Burl Stevens of Cheyenne who were married on the top by the Reverend Charles Hammon.

The first fatal tragedy on Long's Peak occurred September 23, 1884, when Miss Carrie J. Welton died. Carlyle Lamb was her guide. When she and Lamb reached the Keyhole the wind was blowing hard and clouds were gathering, but she refused to turn back. They reached the summit successfully, but Miss Welton was exhausted. Lamb helped her down as far as the Keyhole. It was then midnight and Lamb was forced to leave her in a sheltered spot and go for help. It was five miles to the Lamb cabin. Lamb hurried back with Carlyle, but they were too late. She was dead when they reached her.

Another woman also lost her life on the Peak. Agnes Wolcott Vaille died on January 15, 1925, on her fourth attempt to climb the East Face which is the most dangerous route to the top of the Peak. She climbed steadily for twenty-five hours and when her strength was exhausted, her companion, Walter Kiener, left her to get help. He met a searching party, but when they returned to her, she had died from exhaustion and freezing. One of the searching party had also died. He was Herbert Sortland who had become separated from the party. It was six weeks before his body was discovered. Kiener was badly frozen and lost all but one of his fingertips. He returned, however, to climb the Peak. He has climbed the East Face more than any other person.

The East Face is over 1,700 feet of almost sheer rock; it was not climbed until 1922 when it was climbed by Professor J. W. Alexander. Since then there have been over three hundred climbs and only twenty-two of these climbs were made by women. The danger of the climb is emphasized by the fact that there have been six deaths on the East Face.

Among the most famous early Long's Peak guides were the Reverend E. J. Lamb and his son, Carlyle, Enos A. Mills, Shep Husted, Fred Sprague, and Carl Piltz. Shep Husted, who made perhaps the most climbs to the top of the Peak, guided many famous people. Among them were George Lorimer, a former editor of the *Saturday Evening Post;* Edna Ferber, who climbed with Husted in 1921; Otis Skinner and his family; Will and Charles Mayo; Walt Mason; Charles Evans Hughes; Will Doubleday. In all Shep Husted estimated that he made over eight hundred climbs in the fifty-two years that he spent in the Estes Park region.

It is significant to note that all these guides were Estes Park men and that they were intimately responsible for the growth and development of Estes Park. Since Estes Park has depended upon the tourist trade for its livelihood for so many years and since Long's Peak has drawn so many people to her doors, it is easy to see why Long's Peak has long been considered an integral part of Estes Park. Mountain climbers come very close to "seventh heaven" in Estes Park, for the mountains that ring the Park offer an inviting challenge to them. Long's Peak is the chief attraction to the serious mountain climber, but even the less-agile tourist can have fun scrambling around on Dunraven Mountain, Two Owls, Old Man Mountain, Mt. Olympus, or any of the other picturesquely named mountains that surround the Park.

Accounts of Estes Park written by tourists in the early days present a clear and vivid picture of the joys and trials encountered in a vacation in the Park. The first and, perhaps, most trying ordeal was the day-long, dusty stage coach ride from the plains. It was a worthwhile trip, however, for it was an enchanting sight to emerge from the dark woods and see the green fields and meandering streams.

There were side trips which the visitor could take such as to Lily Lake which was halfway up Long's Peak. Hundreds of orange lilies bloomed on the lake. The lake also served a very practical purpose for a ranchman had dug a ditch from the lake and used the water for irrigation. Every night, however, the beavers dammed the ditch and the rancher had to ride there every morning to tear out the dam.

The fishermen followed beautiful, twisting little streams in pursuit of their sport. Their wanderings might carry them out of Estes Park proper up forbidding Black Cañon Creek, over the moraine to Willow or Moraine Park, or up the Fall River Valley. Wherever they decided to go, they could depend on the excellent fishing. According to one early account published in the *Rocky Mountain News* in 1874, there were over two hundred people in the Park for their health and trout, mostly for trout. Five people who were rated the poorest fishermen took one hundred and twenty-five trout of all sizes from Fall River in six hours. In the book *Fishing with the Fly,* the author, A. Nelson Cheney, described his fishing experiences in Estes Park. According to him, fishing was best from ten until twelve in the morning and around five in the afternoon. Fishing was excellent and it was possible to fill a creel in a short time.

Englishmen were drawn to the Park by stories told by Dunraven and his friends. One of these was A. Pendarves Vivian who contacted Whyte for a hunting trip. He found that while the scenery was beautiful, the hunting was poor. The deer and larger animals had been driven up toward timberline where the less venturesome seldom pursued them.

The Park had been home to the bighorn sheep, elk, deer, and bear. The black bear was the most common although there was an occasional grizzly. Mountain lions were also seen. It was a pity that the hunters and settlers had destroyed or driven all this game away, and in 1913 fifteen enterprising citizens of Estes Park decided to try to bring the elk back to the region. They each pledged a certain amount of money to transport the elk from Granger, Montana, where the elk were rounded up by the United States Forest Service. The elk were then shipped by railroad to Lyons, and from Lyons to Estes Park they were transported in cages built on Stanley Steamers. They were held in a corral northwest of the Stanley Hotel for a time and then freed. Today hunting is permitted in the Estes Park region although not in Rocky Mountain National Park and not in the immediate vicinity of the village of Estes Park.

Vivian was annoyed not only by the fact that the hunting was poor but also by the fact that the road was in such terrible condition. Also the toll charges were three dollars for one vehicle. It is not known if there were two rates, but it seems entirely possible that there were during the tourist season.

For the visitors there were entertainments provided by the hotel men who were determined that there weren't to be any dull moments. Picnics were taken as a matter of course. Other diversions ranged from swimming matches, tennis matches, horse races, shooting contests, open air concerts, baseball games to billiard tournaments with high prizes for the winners. The Estes Park Hotel formed a little lake in front of the hotel and provided several boats for the pleasure of their guests. James at the Elkhorn Lodge organized hunting and fishing parties almost every day for his guests. Then at night a large bonfire was built in front of the Lodge and the guests entertained themselves with songs and stories. These entertainments were typical of those provided by all of the hotels in the region.

Many of the visitors in the early days were from Larimer County. These people generally brought their own tents and camping equipment. However, the hotels were filled with tourists from the East and from Denver. Many Denver people built their own cabins and spent every summer in the Park. It has been said that it would be difficult to find more diversified scenery than there is in Estes Park in the same amount of space elsewhere. Grassy meadows are found all along the streams and these meadows are dotted with little groves of timber. From the gently rolling Park, it is possible to enjoy rugged wild beauty in any of the canyons of the Big Thompson tributaries. It is small wonder that many did not come to enjoy the hunting, fishing, or other sports but came merely to enjoy looking at nature in its most beautiful form.

It became apparent in later years that these beauties of nature stood a good chance of being destroyed. So on January 26, 1915, the Rocky Mountain National Park was created. It was enlarged on February 14, 1917. Thus an area just west of Estes Park was preserved in its natural state for the tourists of today. The Park has an area of 398 square miles or about 255,000 acres. It includes about twenty-nine miles of the Continental Divide and large areas on both the Atlantic and Pacific slopes. It is located in Larimer, Boulder, and Grand counties. Trail Ridge Road carries the visitor through the heart of the Park. The Park is under the supervision of the National Park Service, Department of the Interior. The headquarters of the Park are located in Estes Park.

All the early visitors did not come to the Park for pleasure. In the middle 1870's Estes Park was searched for gold. In the winter of 1875-76 a party of hunters came to the Park. One of the group was a man named Barber who was also a prospector. While hunting he filled his pockets with specimens which he promptly forgot. The next summer a friend, who was an assayer, looked at them and tested a few. One was found to be very rich in gold. The entire piece had been pulverized in making the test, and Barber couldn't remember anything about it except that he had picked it up in Estes Park. Barber and his friend came back to the Park but failed to locate the gold. The next year Barber again returned, and on this trip he told Abner Sprague the story.

Sprague felt that he must have mixed some Boulder County specimens with those from the Park, but Barber was certain that he had not. At any rate he continued to return year after year to hunt for the gold but always in vain.

Bierstadt, the artist, found a piece of quartz in the Loch Vale region. It was shot through with free gold, but the ledges from which it came were never found. The Park was also the starting place for hunts for lost mines west of the divide but little, if anything, ever came of these rumors. There were no mines found in Estes Park although farther to the west there were mines. The old ghost towns of Lulu and Dutch Town in the Rocky Mountain National Park were located near these mines.

The United States Geographical Survey which was more commonly known as the Hayden Survey became interested in the Estes Park region in 1873. The Survey was headed by Professor F. V. Hayden, who described the Park as the largest of the cozy nooks hidden in the mountains. Another member of the Survey was the famed pioneer photographer, William H. Jackson, who was in charge of the Photographic Division of the Survey. The Hayden Survey was very influential in advertising the Park. An official description of the region was included in the important annual reports of the United States Geological and Geographical Survey. Even more important, however, were the pictures taken by W. H. Jackson. His work has been challenged by few in beauty and composition.

Many books and pamphlets were written to acquaint the would-be traveler with the advantages of a vacation in Estes Park. Among them were the advertising pamphlets put out with the compliments of the Burlington Railroad giving all manner of information such as the names of the mountains, the side trips that could be taken, accommodations, and the rates. George A. Crofutt, who was responsible for a number of tourist guides, wrote the *New Overland Tourist and Pacific Coast Guide* and the *Grip-Sack Guide of Colorado*. In both of these books he was most fluent in his praises of Estes Park. He described the Park as "one of those places seldom found in the mountains where all the greatest attractions can be enjoyed within easy reach from excellent hotel accommodations." J. S. Perky wrote a book called *Homes and Mines.* According to Mr. Perky everything was excellent in the Park—fishing, camping, hunting, accommodations, and mail service. In consequence of this sort of publicity there were no less than two thousand people in the Park during the summer of 1879.

The first hotel accommodations, as noted before, were kept by Griff Evans. The other ranchers — the MacGregors, the Fergusons, the Jameses, the Lambs, and the Spragues — were also hotel men. By far the most commodious hotel in the early days was the Estes Park Hotel which had fifty rooms. The hotel was richly furnished and efficiently managed for a number of years by Alexander Stetson whom Dunraven had persuaded to leave New York for Estes Park. According to the *Denver Republican* in 1881,

> Tourists seeking new scenes in nature could not do better than to visit this famous nook of the Rockies and epicures hunting a mountain retreat where they can live with all the table delicacies and luxuries of a metropolis can find such an institution in Estes Park.

Another paper remarked that Stetson was keeping his hotel in true Parisian style and serving all the "tony dishes." The rates at the Estes Park Hotel during that summer of 1881 were four dollars per day or fifteen to seventeen dollars per week.

After the turn of the century many new hotels were opened. Among them were the Wind River Lodge, Long's Peak Inn, Lake View, Manford Hotel, Hupp Hotel, and the Rustic. In 1909 the famous Stanley Hotel was completed. Several years prior to this, Sprague sold his interest in Sprague's Lodge to J. D. Stead. The Lodge then became known as Stead's Ranch and Lodge. It wasn't until 1910 that Sprague returned to Estes Park to build and manage the new Sprague's Lodge.

In 1911 the Estes Park Hotel burned. C. E. Lester had been the manager for a number of years and when it was destroyed, he bought the Rustic and renamed it Lester's. That same year a number of new hotels were established.

72

They were the Brinwood Hotel, Hewes-Kirkwood, Colum-
bines, Fall River Lodge, Lewiston, Copeland Lake Lodge,
Baldpate Inn, and the Big Thompson Hotel. The Horseshoe
Inn and the Timberline Hotel had been established in 1908.
Perhaps the most unusual of these hotels is the Baldpate Inn
owned and operated by the Mace family. The Inn is located
on the road to Long's Peak and is famous as the setting for
the book, *Seven Keys to Baldpate,* and for its Key Room
which contains keys of every sort from all over the world.

This was Estes Park as the tourist saw it. Small wonder
that such famous people as General Frederick Funston,
Arthur Scribner, Philip Aston Rollins, and Jane Addams
came to visit. William Allen White and F. O. Stanley found
it so enchanting that they made it their summer home. The
number of tourists who have visited Estes Park has grown
from the few who explored the Park with Joel Estes to over
1,200,000 each year. Caring for the visitors has become a
leading industry in Estes Park and too much emphasis cannot be directed to their influence on the lives of the people
in the Park. The village of Estes Park would never have
been built nor would it have developed into the thriving
little community it is today if it weren't for the tourist trade.

The Village of Estes Park

The center of Park life today is the bustling little village of Estes Park. The village is comparatively new in the history of the Park since it was not built until 1905. The establishment of the village marks the end of the pioneer period in Estes Park and the beginning of a modern Estes Park, but before this transition could take place there were two large real estate transfers. The first was the purchase by C. H. Bond and the Estes Park Town Company of the John T. Cleave property at the junction of the Fall River with the Big Thompson. The second large transfer of property was from the Earl of Dunraven to B. D. Sanborn of Greeley, Colorado, and F. O. Stanley of Newton, Massachusetts.

On August 24, 1905, C. H. Bond and his associates, J. B. Anderson, W. L. Beckfield, J. Y. Munson, and F. M. Wright, formed the Estes Park Town Company. The company was formed for the purpose of purchasing land and platting the town site of Estes Park. Several of the associates had previously purchased the Cleave Ranch with the intention of making Estes Park the prettiest resort in the West. The Cleave Ranch was the logical location for the town site since it was centrally located and since the post office, school, and other important buildings were already built on the property. Cleave received $8,000 for the quarter section of land which comprised the ranch.

Cornelius H. Bond, who had the foresight to see a thriving little village in the Park, was a former Ohio resident. He came west to Loveland in 1879. He was a public official for a number of years, sheriff for two terms, state legislator for three terms, and a member of the school board for a number of years. He was always interested in the Park, and it will be remembered that he was largely responsible for the building of the Big Thompson Canyon Road. After the village was built, he moved to the Park and engaged in the real estate business until his death in May, 1931.

Lord Dunraven and his friend, Lord Barrymore, who had acquired an interest in the property, finally agreed to sell their land in Estes Park in 1907. For several years prior to 1907, people had tried to buy the property. Among them was Guy La Coste who had homesteaded up Wind River. He was a former newspaper man who gave up the field of journalism to build and operate the Wind River Lodge. In 1904 he went to England to persuade Dunraven to sell the land. Dunraven seemed rather favorable to the idea at the time but he did not actually relinquish the property until 1907 when he sold it to Sanborn and Stanley.

Sanborn arranged the purchase of Dunraven's holdings in the Park through Frank Prestidge who was Dunraven's agent in Denver. A day or so after Sanborn made the deal, he discovered that F. O. Stanley was also interested in the property. Sanborn met with Stanley and Stanley agreed that for half interest in the company which Sanborn had formed he would build a hotel and a light plant. The company was called the Estes Park Development Company; it is still operating today. Land is being developed as there is a demand for new residential areas. Carl B. Sanborn, son of B. D. Sanborn, who died in 1914, is the president of the company.

Sanborn and Stanley purchased about 6,400 acres of deeded land and about 600 acres which was in litigation. The purchase also included the Estes Park Hotel, the Earl's cottage, stables, dairy, and the Country Club House. The reported price for all of this property was in the neighborhood of $80,000, and the final payment was made in June, 1908, when the property was formally transferred to Sanborn and Stanley.

The purchase of Dunraven's interests in Estes Park was the result of a lifelong dream of B. D. Sanborn. His desire was to make the Park the most popular resort in the country and he was especially interested in encouraging the construction of summer homes and road building within the Park. Sanborn owned two cottages in the Park and both Bierstadt and Bear Lakes prior to the purchase from Dunraven. He had also secured water rights in order to provide electricity for the Park. Since his summer home was in Estes Park, he was in a position to know the problems and possibilities of developing Estes Park as a resort. He hoped that several thousand people would take up residence in the Park within several years. Although development was possibly not as quick as he had hoped, through the following years thousands have made it, at least, their summer home.

The purchase of the Park was thought by many to mean that a large storage reservoir would be built in the main part of the Park. Sanborn felt that although it was a worthwhile project there was neither enough money nor enough water to warrant such a reservoir. He declared that the government would have to spend millions bringing additional water to the Park before such a lake could be built. These were prophetic words since Lake Estes now occupies the ground considered for the lake. Lake Estes has been constructed as a part of the Colorado-Big Thompson Reclamation Project which has spent literally millions to bring additional water from the western slope to Estes Park.

F. O. Stanley was no less interested in the development, progress, and affairs of Estes Park than Sanborn. Possibly he felt a certain sense of gratitude to the Park for it was in Estes Park that he regained his health. Stanley had been ordered to come to a high, dry climate because he was a tuberculosis patient. He was fifty-four years old and weighed a little over one hundred pounds at the time. The doctors had given him only a few months to live but told him that if he came to Colorado he might live a year. He lived for thirty-seven years after he came to the Park and became known as the "Grand Old Man of Estes Park."

Stanley and his wife came to Denver in June, 1903, where they heard about Estes Park. They decided to go there, so Stanley arranged for his wife and her maid to go by train to Lyons and then by stage coach to the Park.

Stanley was determined to drive his Stanley Steamer to the Park. The automobile had been invented and manufactured by Stanley and his twin brother, and he had had one sent to Denver for his use. He had planned to have a companion on the trip but the man failed to arrive at the meeting place so Stanley started off alone across unknown roads. When he finally arrived at Welsh's stage station at Lyons, he requested a companion for the rest of the trip but was refused because Welsh did not want to sacrifice a man in the Steamer. Stanley went on up the North St. Vrain road and arrived in the Park in one hour and fifty minutes. He promptly called Welsh from Sam Service's store but Welsh refused to believe him until Service assured him that Stanley was really in the Park.

Freeman Oscar Stanley was about five feet ten inches tall; in later years he had white hair and wore sideburns. He was considered by those who knew him to be a genius. He and his brother, Francis E. Stanley, developed a superior method of coating photographic plates with a sensitive dry emulsion. When the Stanley Dry Plates were sold to the George Eastman Company in 1904, the brothers turned their talents to developing the Stanley Steamer. Stanley was also an architect, designer, engineer, teacher, and a profound student of political economy. The Stanley Hotel was constructed from his own plans. He was also a wonderful violinist and from the time he was ten, his hobby was making violins. He developed some new processes for making them.

The hotel which Stanley had agreed to build was opened in 1909. It had taken two years to construct. Stanley had considered naming the hotel "the Dunraven Hotel" but *The Mountaineer*, which was the Estes Park newspaper, protested loudly. The name Dunraven seemed to conjure only unpleasant memories so the paper suggested that the hotel be called the Stanley Hotel. Stanley offered a ten dollar prize for a hotel name but he finally acquiesced to the popular demand and allowed the hotel to be called the Stanley. The hotel was formally opened by a convention of the State Pharmacist Association which convened June

22, 1909. The management of the hotel was under the supervision of Alfred Lambourne of New York City who remained with the hotel until 1921. The hotel originally had eighty-eight rooms but cottages were planned to supplement the hotel's capacity. When the tourist response indicated that more room was needed, the Stanley Manor was built near the original hotel.

Work was started on the hydro-electric plant about the same time as the hotel was being built because Stanley had planned an all electric kitchen for the hotel. The plant was originally intended as a private enterprise to supply electricity to the hotel only. However, the town and other hotels were anxious to have electric power so the plant was soon furnishing power for the Park.

Stanley did much to justify his name as the "Grand Old Man of Estes Park." He gave property valued at $8,000 to Estes Park for a new school building. When the village built a sewer system, Stanley donated land for a disposal plant on the Stanley Meadows. The Stanleys continued to spend their summers in the Park even after they sold their holdings in Estes Park. They sold the Stanley Hotel and Manor, the power plant, and approximately 2,750 acres of land to the Stanley Corporation in 1926. C. H. Bond handled the sale; the price was rumored to exceed half a million dollars.

Mrs. Flora J. R. Stanley died in Estes Park in July, 1939, at the age of ninety-one years. Mr. Stanley died in Newton, Massachusetts, in 1940. They had no children. Stanley is still well remembered in the Park as the man who brought the modern tourist business to Estes Park.

Until the Estes Park Town Company platted the town site there wasn't a village in the Park. In 1892 the only two buildings that could be found on what was to be the main street were John Cleave's frame house and an 8'x10' frame post office. By 1904 there were a number of buildings on Elkhorn Avenue. F. P. Clatworthy, an early day businessman, wrote a vivid picture of the first business houses in the village. According to his account the main street was a road bordered mainly by pastures and barbed wire fences.

At the east end of the street on the south side near the present Hayden Realty Office was the Samuel Service general merchandise store which was the original W. T. Parke store. Next to the Service store was the blacksmith shop run by Jim Boyd who was Service's brother-in-law. Some distance west was located Parke's photo shop. Across the road on the corner which is now occupied by the Chez Jay was a small general store run by Elizabeth Foot and Jenny Chapin who were two businesslike young women. To the west of their store was the post office. On west of the post office "Lord Cornwallis" Rogers, a well-educated Englishman, had a cabin and a pump which he used for photographic purposes. Frank Grubb managed Cantwell's stage barn which stood at the extreme west end of the town on the south side.

On the north side of the street at the west end, the Johnson Brothers had a meat market built of logs. Coming east the next building was the Cleave home and next to it was the community building which was the largest building in the town. It served not only as a church and school but also as a meeting hall for public gatherings. Later it was used for a dance hall, Odd Fellows Hall, and a movie theatre. Next to the community building Clatworthy established a photographic studio in 1905 on the present site of the Estes Park Bank. The last building on the north side of the street was John Manford's home.

Until the Town Company had their surveys made by Abner Sprague, many people were living in tents waiting to buy lots. Needless to say these prospective villagers were agreeably surprised when they discovered that the top price for a twenty-five foot lot was only fifty dollars instead of the two hundred dollars they had expected to pay. In fact, at the east end of town lots were only thirty-five dollars. Some were even offered at a cheaper rate. Dr. W. J. Workman of Ashland, Kansas, later ruefully admitted that he had refused to give twenty-five dollars for a corner lot on Elkhorn Avenue. Again needless to say, this was 1905. Today such a lot, if available, would cost $10,000 to $15,000. However, the title to the land which the Town Company held was not clear. They had to send a man to England to visit Dunraven and spend $3,000 to get a clear title. It will be remembered that Cleave had obtained this land from Dunraven. Those who bought lots in the new town went ahead with their building and hoped for the best.

1905 was, indeed, a year of building and many new businesses were opened. Clatworthy established his studio in a building that was fourteen by thirty feet and had the first real store window in the Park. It was a four by five foot glass window. Over the store was a sign which said "Everything for the Tourist"; besides his photography studio, Clatworthy had the first soda fountain and also sold leather goods, eggs, and fruits. Among the other businesses that were started was a shoe repair shop, a bakery, a barber shop, and a livery. Julian Johnson built the first laundry which was later taken over by Ralph McDonald. George and Ben Johnson built a small stage station. A weekly newspaper was started. However, when a year's subscription had been collected and a few issues printed, the publisher skipped town.

With so many people moving to the Park, it became increasingly difficult to find room and board. Therefore it was not long before hotels were built in the village proper. The first ones to be constructed were the Hupp Hotel and the Manford House. The Hupp was built in 1906 by Mrs. Josie Hupp. It contained twenty-three rooms with steam heat and had baths with hot and cold water. The Manford House, which was located on the corner of Elkhorn Avenue and Moraine Drive, had room for fifty. Mrs. Hupp later purchased the Manford House.

By 1908 the village had grown enough to warrant the organization of a bank. So the Estes Park Bank was organized with F. O. Stanley as president and J. D. Stead and C. H. Bond as vice-presidents. The bank building was located opposite the Hupp Hotel on a corner lot.

That same year an Estes Park newspaper, *The Mountaineer*, was published. One man remarked that "this place is getting too civilized" when he heard that the Park was to have a paper. The first three issues were not printed in the Park but by the time the fourth issue was put out, the paper had moved to the Park. Gordon Smith was the editor. The paper was a summer weekly and passed out of existence after the first summer. The *Estes Park Trail*, which is the Estes Park paper of today, was begun in 1912. It was owned and edited by J. Y. Munson who was also the editor of the *Berthoud Bulletin*.

1900 saw the first long distance telephone connection between Estes Park and the world. There was no local exchange until 1908 and all the calls went through Loveland. By 1908, however, the lines had been purchased from the Colorado Telephone Company by an Estes Park company and a local exchange was built with toll lines to Loveland and Lyons. At those points calls were connected to the Colorado Telephone Company lines which gave direct connection to Colorado, Wyoming, New Mexico, and Utah. There were fifty subscribers to this exchange in 1908.

The Estes Park volunteer fire department was organized in January, 1907, with R. J. Tallent as president and Dr. Homer James as chief. The first fire house was located on the corner behind the Bank.

Among the companies which were formed in the early history of the village was the Estes Park Water Company and the Estes Park Electric Light and Power Company which were incorporated in 1908. The water company was formed by F. O. Stanley, Donald MacGregor, H. E. James, J. Y. Munson, and C. H. Bond to furnish the residents of Estes Park with water from Black Cañon Creek. This company served the community until it was dissolved in 1930. Stanley with Bond, Munson, and S. W. Sherman formed the light and power company to build the hydro-electric plant on Fall River. This plant, which was located about a mile from the post office on the road to Horseshoe Park, supplied the Park with power.

The first school district in Estes Park was created in 1883 at the request of eleven petitioners. There were fifteen children of school age in the Park at the time. For three years school was held in the Elkhorn Lodge and Dr. Judson Ellis was the first teacher. He was paid forty dollars a month salary plus fifteen dollars for board. Then in 1886 a school house was built. The building originally stood near the present bank but with families living all over the Park, the school was frequently moved. Until 1905 when regular desks and seats were purchased, the pupils used long shelf desks with soap and cracker boxes for seats. Another school house was built in 1906 and the staff increased to three teachers. By 1911 high school subjects were taught by one teacher.

In 1908 *The Mountaineer* observed that there were certain things a town needed to meet the demands of civilization. "They are: a school, a church, a bank, and a newspaper." Estes Park had everything except the church. Church services had been held irregularly at various ranches from the time of Joel Estes' residence in the Park. When the school was settled in the village near the Cleaves, services were held there by the Reverend E. J. Lamb. Other pioneer ministers in the Park were the Reverend E. L. Baldwin, the Reverend C. H. Walker, and the Reverend A. Griffith. Visiting ministers also held services in the resort hotels. Then in June, 1908, the Reverend John Knox Hall and the Reverend R. G. Knox came to Estes Park to organize a Presbyterian Church. The building was erected that same year at a cost of $4,000. Hall cared for the church until Knox was called.

The village remained unincorporated until 1917. Then an election was held on April 3 to determine if the town should be incorporated. There were 317 residents at the time; of these 73 voted for incorporation and 12 against. Dr. Roy Weist became the first mayor.

The growth from a home and a post office to a thriving business and residential center was due to the foresight and planning of men such as Bond, Stanley, and Sanborn. It is to the vision of these early businessmen and their friends that the Village of today owes its existence.

Estes Park Today

The Village of Estes Park has grown steadily in size and in civic improvements during the years that have followed its founding in 1905. The Estes Park region has also witnessed several improvements of national as well as local interest such as the creation of the Rocky Mountain National Park and the Colorado-Big Thompson Reclamation Project. According to the latest census the permanent population of the Village is 1,590. Precinct 37, which is the voting district immediately surrounding the Village, has a population of 2,569; but during the summer, in the area which compares roughly with that of Precinct 37, the population increases to about 45,000. The reasons for the growth of both the permanent and transient population are several. Probably the regional development is responsible for influencing the permanent population since the headquarters for both the Colorado-Big Thompson Project and the Rocky Mountain National Park are located in the Village. The tourists are responsible, of course, for the increase in population during the summer, and the growth in the number of summer visitors can be traced to the increased knowledge of the Park and to the increased accommodations. However, despite, or perhaps because of, the civic and federal developments, Estes Park still retains the fascinating flavor of the Rocky Mountain West.

The Village attained the modern aspect that it has today rather slowly. In fact, it wasn't until 1921 that the town seriously considered its responsibility in repairing and improving the streets. When it was finally decided to purchase a plow and grader, provision was also made for placing and repairing a hitching post at the post office! Elkhorn Avenue was not graded nor were gutters installed until 1926, but in 1932 the present pavement on the Avenue was opened with a celebration.

Even before the physical needs of the Village were considered, the cultural needs of the community were realized. One of the primary needs was recognized when the Estes Park Library was founded by the Estes Park Woman's Club in 1916. The first library room was located in the school which offered the Club space if they would care for the school library. Mrs. C. H. Bond donated her services as librarian, and the library was started with 262 books. In 1922 the present library building was built in the little park located on Elkhorn Avenue; it was financed by contributions not only from the residents but also from the summer visitors. Then in 1935 Mrs. Pieter Hondius built and furnished the attractive reading room as a memorial to her husband. The library, which welcomes residents and visitors alike, now has a collection of some 7,262 volumes.

The spiritual life of the community has centered around the several churches which represent various denominations. The two churches which have conducted the most vigorous building programs are the Community Church of the Rockies and the Church of Our Lady of the Mountains. The Community Church, which is located on Elkhorn Avenue, was completed in 1939 and the Church of Our Lady was finished only a short time ago. It stands near the Big Thompson Road overlooking Lake Estes.

In 1939 the Village had new visitors of a type not generally associated with a normal community for some bears had come down from the Rocky Mountain National Park to see what was going on in Estes Park. When the Town Board met to decide how properly to greet the new arrivals, one board member declared that window peeking by an inquisitive bear was both an unnerving experience and a menace to happy home life. The *Estes Park Trail* rose to the emergency and declared that the *Trail* stood ready to do its part in the current crisis and if the Board considered it necessary, they would print pamphlets to be distributed

84

by airplane or other means. The Board seems to have rejected the *Trail's* offer. Instead the Board members and local peace officers were armed and given orders to kill bears on sight. The next week one of the visiting bruins was shot. This ended the bear menace.

As the Village grew both the school and the post office found that their limited space was not adequate. The present grade school was erected in 1915, and the civic auditorium which was built in 1926 was used for high school classes. In 1939 a new junior and senior high school was constructed. It was built of reinforced concrete and tile and was connected to the civic auditorium. About five hundred students are enrolled in the Estes Park schools at the present. The new post office was constructed in 1941 and the old post office building located in the Park on Elkhorn Avenue is used for city offices.

Other civic improvements have included new zoning laws and a new Chamber of Commerce building. In 1946 the first serious attention was given to the need for zoning rules. Until that time very little had been done in the way of planning for the growth of the Village. In 1947 the regulations were passed which separate the commercial and residential sections. The Chamber of Commerce building which is located on the main street for the convenience of visitors was dedicated in September, 1950.

In keeping with the new modern aspect of Estes Park is the airport located two miles southeast of the Village. The present facilities include only a hangar and one north-south runway but improvement plans are being made. For a time Estes Park had a regular airline called the Estes Scenic Airways owned by V. C. Rasmussen. In 1946 the Park was the convention headquarters for the Sportsman Pilot's Association. They put a stamp of approval on Estes Park as a vacation center for the flying public.

Perhaps one of the most interesting summer entertainments is the annual Roof-Top Rodeo. It was first held in 1907 as a real community affair, but during the war years it was not conducted. The rodeo has been sponsored by the Summer Residents Association and the Roof-Top Rodeo

Association which was formed in 1941; the Roof-Top Rodeo has been held under their direction since then. The Rodeo is held southeast of the Village.

When the Rocky Mountain National Park was created in 1915, an area was preserved as nearly as possible in its natural state. Because of the easy access to it from Estes Park and Grand Lake, it immediately became a mecca for lovers of scenic beauty. During the first year 30,000 visitors were counted. That number has grown steadily and in 1950, 1,265,988 people visited the National Park. The headquarters for the vast organization of the Park is located in the Village. The duties and activities of these men are wide and varied and very important to the people of Estes Park for the rangers are responsible for the only area in the region which is to be kept relatively unchanged. It is necessary to qualify the word "unchanged" for certain changes are required to provide the visitor access to the Park area. However, the National Park was not created merely as a recreation area but as a sample of natural landscape and the responsibility of the Park Rangers is to see that only those changes are made that are necessary.

The duties of the Park Rangers are virtually unlimited. They are in charge of fire control, rescue service, insect control, public camp grounds, weather studies, and roads within the Park. They are also law enforcement agents and, since any crimes committed in the Park are federal offenses, trials are held at the Park Headquarters with a United States Commissioner from the United States District Court as judge. A bear skin hanging on the wall of their office is evidence of the Park Rangers' skill as detectives. Eight months from the time that the bear was shot in the Park where hunting is illegal, the hunter was on trial. He was apprehended because someone heard a single shot and through the months that followed the Rangers quietly pieced the evidence together that led to the hunter's conviction.

Although hunting is illegal, fishing is permitted in the Park; it is necessary to have a Colorado fishing license although it is federal property. So another activity of the Park Service is to stock the streams with fish which they obtain

86

from the fish hatchery on Fall River. The Park Rangers are also responsible for checking with the fishermen to see if they have legal size trout.

The Park Naturalist and his staff are responsible for the interpretation of the Park story to the summer visitors. Illustrated talks are given in the evenings during the summer season not only in the museums which they maintain but also in the hotels in the region. Guided hikes from an hour to a day in length are conducted to acquaint the visitor with certain views of nature which might otherwise be missed. While the Park Rangers do not guide mountain climbers, visitors who are planning mountain hikes are urged to check with them regarding routes, conditions, and proposed time of return since they are responsible for rescuing anyone who becomes lost or is injured.

During the winter the Park Rangers supervise the skiing which is held in Hidden Valley. They open the Trail Ridge Road as far as upper Hidden Valley every weekend during the season which lasts roughly from Thanksgiving to May 30th. Skiing is very good in this area and a temporary tow is operated for the convenience of the skiers. The main area is the Big Drift and there are also trails from upper Hidden Valley to the lower valley. There are numerous cross country trips that are possible over trails which are generally used in the summer. The Park Rangers are on duty at the skiing area throughout the season. Occasionally summer ski carnivals are held but these are not under the auspices of the Park Rangers. Snow is hauled down to Old Man Mountain just outside the Village and jumping contests are held.

Throughout the summer and winter the Rocky Mountain National Park Headquarters stands ready to serve the visitors. However, it should not be forgotten that their primary job is to guard the Park area in order to preserve it in its natural state.

As early as 1889 the necessity of obtaining additional water for irrigation of the dry, eastern plains was recognized. In that year a survey was made of the possibility of bringing water from the headwaters of the Colorado River near Grand

Lake, and fifty years later the actual work was begun. Although the primary purpose of the Colorado-Big Thompson Reclamation Project is to provide the plains area with the water that is needed for irrigation, there are several other purposes which will be served. Hydro-electric power will be generated and one of the power plants is being built in Estes Park. Another phase of the project is the storage of water for the western slope. The work that has been done in the Estes Park area is only a small part of the total project which includes dams and lakes on the Blue River, Colorado River, North Fork of the Colorado River, and various foothill regions.

Water from Grand Lake emerges in Estes Park from the Prospect Mountain Tunnel. It first passes through the power plant and then enters Lake Estes which is a man-made lake formed behind Olympus Dam. From this lake, water is released to the foothill reservoirs where it is held until needed for irrigation. For the average visitor the most striking feature of the project in Estes Park is the lake which covers 163 acres in the heart of the Park. The water was first turned into the lake during the last of November, 1948, and since that time it has been open for fishing and boating. It is an extremely attractive lake and new homes are being built which overlook it.

The construction headquarters for the Colorado-Big Thompson Reclamation Project are located in Estes Park; many of the employees of the project live in the Reclamation village which is located on the edge of town. These residents have greatly increased the population of Estes Park, and this is a permanent change since a staff will always be located in the Park to maintain the power plant even after the construction work has been completed.

The Colorado-Big Thompson Reclamation Project might be considered the climax of the modern development of Estes Park. Yet Estes Park today is a series of contrasts between the old and the new. The Rocky Mountain National Park has preserved the Park as it was in its natural state before human occupation, while the Reclamation project has modified nature to benefit human life. The Village is also a series of compromises between the modern and the old. The homes, business buildings, and hotels contrast the rustic with the modern. The Park people are consciously striving to retain the best of both periods. It is this combination of old and new which is Estes Park today.

SELECTED BIBLIOGRAPHY

Bird, Isabella L., *A Lady's Life in the Rocky Mountains.* London: John Murray, 1880.

Carothers, June E., "The Early History of Estes Park." Unpublished Master's thesis, University of Denver, Denver, 1950.

Chittenden, Hiram Martin, *The American Fur Trade of the Far West,* 2 vols. New York: The Press of the Pioneers, Inc., 1935.

Estes, Milton, "Memoirs of Estes Park," *Colorado Magazine,* XVI (July, 1939), 121-132.

Estes Park Trail

Foscue, E. J. and Quam, L. O., *Estes Park: Resort in the Rockies.* Dallas: University Press, 1949.

Lamb, E. J., *Miscellaneous Meditations.* n.p.: The Publishers' Press Room and Bindery Company, n.d.

——————, *Memories of the Past and Thoughts of the Future.* n.p.: Press of the United Brethren Publishing House, 1906.

Mills, Enos A., *The Rocky Mountain National Park.* Garden City: Doubleday Page and Company, 1924.

——————, *The Story of Estes Park.* Estes Park, Colorado: published by the author, 1917.

——————, *The Story of Estes Park and a Guide Book.* Denver, Colorado: Outdoor Life Publishing Company, 1905.

Nesbit, Paul W., *Long's Peak.* Colorado Springs, Colorado: Out West Printing and Stationery Company, 1946.

Sage, Rufus, *Rocky Mountain Life.* Dayton, Ohio: Edward Canby, n.d.

Sprague, Abner E., "Estes-Rocky Mountain National Park." Colorado State Historical Museum, MSS XXVI-38.

——————, "Reminiscences of a Pioneer," Colorado State Historical Museum, MSS XXVI-37.

Toll, Roger W., *Mountaineering in the Rocky Mountain National Park.* Washington, D. C.: Government Printing Office, 1919.

Wyndham-Quin, Windham Thomas, Earl of Dunraven, *Past Times and Pastimes.* London: Hodder and Staughton, 1922.

CPSIA information can be obtained
at www.ICGtesting.com
Printed in the USA
BVHW050736100523
663912BV00019B/19